DULCIE
DISHES THE DIRT

Also by Sue Limb

UP THE GARDEN PATH
DULCIE DOMUM'S BAD HOUSEKEEPING*
MORE BAD HOUSEKEEPING*
SHEEP'S EYES & HOGWASH

*available from Fourth Estate

DULCIE DISHES THE DIRT
Yet More Bad Housekeeping

Sue Limb

FOURTH ESTATE · *London*

For Jenny Baynes
and
Jonathan James-Moore

First published in Great Britain in 1994 by
Fourth Estate Limited
289 Westbourne Grove
London W11 2QA

A catalogue record for this book is available from the
British Library

ISBN 1 85702 236 X

Typeset by York House Typographic Ltd, London
Printed in Great Britain by Cox & Wyman Limited, Reading

one

Her thumbs still sore from the ceaseless thrumming of the steam-loom (or Throbbin' Robin as it was known in Berpsover) Fanny scurried through the beetling dusk to Laurel Villas, a development of sombre but grand houses on the outskirts of town. Here, at number sixteen, lodged Gertrude Lillywhite, Fanny's erstwhile English mistress who had initiated her into the mysteries of European Literature. Indeed, it was Gertrude's dog-eared Bacon which lay next to Milton under Fanny's threadbare pillow back at Blunkett Row.

From Gertrude's attic window, on a clear day, you could see beyond the grimy slag-heaps of Berpsover, to the towering grandeur of Dudley Moor and, on the horizon, the twin peaks of Gran Tor, the shivering mountain, worshipped as Great Earth Mother, millennia before, by the local iron-age tribe the Lagerloutae.

Gertrude waited at her window, anxiously fingering an unlit cigarette she had rolled from a few pale wisps of Hardacre's Thick Old Shag: not so much a vice as a badge of emancipation. Would Fanny never come? Gertrude shivered and drew her thin brown twinset protectively across her breasts – which, despite the slender fragility of her frame, quivered with unexpected opulence like a brace of Buff Orpingtons gone broody and big with egg.

Hope that publisher will find this an encouraging beginning. Intoxicated by knowledge that Spouse and children are in Scotland and that I may indulge in two days' undisturbed titillation. Will pitch new bonkbuster somewhere between *The Rainbow* and the *Sun*. (Possible title? Previous – Russian – bonkbuster to be published soon, entitled *Birches*. Publisher confident of good sales among Old School Tie Brigade.)

Old college friend Alice rang at Christmas – from the Alhambra, blast her – to recommend Sapphic slant to new book. Told her of ex-lover Tom's recent taunting reappearance at bookshop, after many months' separation, to request that I dedicate a book 'To Lucy' for him. Treated me as if a stranger and then departed without a backward look. Felt stirred and shaken. Convinced it was a cruel device to emphasise Tom has deserted me, abandoned me, nay told me to get stuffed. *Ariadne auf Paxo.*

'Dulcie,' commented Alice after hearing this sad tale, 'what you need is a new woman in your life.' Hence Fanny and Gertrude.

Privately convinced, however, that unusual sweetness of present few days caused by the departure from my life of everybody whatsoever. But back to Bustbonker.

At last! Fanny's musical step sounded in the street. Gertrude fled to her landing, the blood booming in her ears, and hovered whilst, below, Mrs Grimestop the landlady admitted the familiar Fanny. As the girl ascended, she raised her divine eyes which, at the sight of Gertrude, glowed like the sulphurous flares which sometimes gleamed above the headshaft of the Guscott and Pikelet Colliery.

Gertrude admired the tendrils of Fanny's hair, which snaked about her neck like indolent whips, and the stately tremor of her bosom. Curiously enough, Fanny was even more generously endowed than Gertrude. Though barely seventeen, her queenly form, majestic but modest in its dark mill clothing, resembled nothing so much as Gran Tor itself.

Suspect this new oeuvre may necessitate the invention of an exotic form of pre-war corsetry: the Bonkbustbodice.

The moment Gertrude's door was closed upon their precious privacy, the girls fell into as close an embrace as was permitted by their anatomies. Withdrawing slightly, though, Fanny scrutinised her friend's fair face.

'Why, Gertrude!' she whispered. 'Is something amiss?'

Phone rings. Heart leaps up and sticks to tonsils. It is not Spouse as I rang him an hour ago to ensure All Well in North. Can it be – lurch foolishly to phone and seize.

'Oh, Dulcie! This is Elaine – you know – I live opposite. Do you mind coming over for a moment? Only I've done something a bit stupid.' Agree and avidly anticipate. Elaine hitherto unexplored, but who knows? This could be the advent of a bosom chum.

two

but Fanny detected an unusual quiver in Gertrude's well-upholstered nether lip . . .

Comb hair (consigned to set-aside for period of Spouse's absence) and depart.

Cross road, suppressing selfish qualm about exactly what sort of help may be required of me. So far, relationship with Elaine confined to distant nods and Christmas cards – though she did provide me with a haven once when I locked myself out. She may, for all I know, be drunk, mad or, worst of all, a bore.

Sobriety and sanity, however, prevail, and I am installed on long, low, immaculate cream sofa (one of the perks of the childless) and supplied with tea and home-made cake.

'It's a long story, Dulcie,' she begins, 'but it all started when Marc left me for Heidi Finsterhorn.' Express incredulity and outrage.

Marc had in the past often been absent but it turned out apparently that he was not so much Away on Business but Off on the Job. The feckless Fraulein Finsterhorn had seduced him at a confectionery conference in Berne, resulting in many an illicit Swiss Roll in her apartment overlooking the Schlockersee.

Elaine pauses to wipe her eyes on recently ironed hand-kerchief. Amazed that a woman living alone should bother to iron handkerchiefs for herself. Spouse has only been absent for three days, but already I have sunk into Yahoo existence. The twisted corpses of discarded bath towels lie strewn across the bathroom floor like the aftermath of some appalling massacre. Half-finished tins of tuna fester on the kitchen table, and if I had a Nine Men's Morris it would not only be filled up with mud but sadly in need of an MOT.

So, in short, necessary to visit rather than be visited. Begin to warm to Elaine, especially as she appears, amidst other tactful details, to possess an even smaller bust than myself.

Her story is briefly told: skint after the desertion of Marc, Elaine advertised for a lodger, and but two hours earlier had interviewed a software specialist, one Tony Sharp ('Call me Tone').

'And the trouble was, Dulcie, he somehow managed to intimidate me into offering him the room even though I didn't really take to him. And he wants to move in on Monday!' Recognise this syndrome, and sympathise. 'What can I do?'

'Er . . .'

Luckily my earlier indulgence in tuna (dolphin-friendly, but presumably tuna-hostile) had refreshed that part of the brain dealing with ingenious excuses – not a part, alas, much exercised these days. We decide to tell Tone that, five minutes after his departure, I appeared on Elaine's doorstep demanding sanctuary from my brutal wife-beating husband.

Elaine convinced of my genius, and we spend the next hour over Sancerre and salted almonds, embellishing details of Spouse's supposed atrocities. Circumstantial detail always convincing, and we have such a good time, begin to think perhaps I should leave Spouse and go to live with her anyway. The way she continually refills my glass and laughs at my jokes suggests she may be the wife I have always wanted.

Eventually lurch home, though ready to reappear in my role of battered wife if necessary.

Attempt to get back into novel, but seem to have locked myself out. Manage only one sentence before falling on the sofa in a doze.

('Fanny,' said Gertrude with a quiet composure that filled Fanny with dread, 'I'm afraid I have bad news, my dear.')

Find myself watching video of *Some Like It Hot* and realise that Marilyn Monroe would have been perfect as Fanny Hoddle in the screen version of my latest work – *Twixt the Rainbow and the Sun*. Suppose we shall have to make do with Samantha Fox.

Spend the night wondering if *Between the Rainbow*, etc would be better. *Twixt* sounds too chocolate-boxy, somehow.

Spouse and children return from Scotland, and Harriet throws off my maternal embrace with 'Ugh, gruesome!' Fear that this indicates the end of some kind of era. Sorely tempted to return to Elaine's salted almonds.

three

'MUMMEE! I WANT TO write a letter to the Queen!'

'Never mind the Queen. Write to Aunt Elspeth first.'

'No! The Queen! The Queen!'

'The blinking Queen didn't give you a Fuzzy Felt set!'

'Don't say the blinking Queen! You mustn't swear! I'm nearly a Brownie! And anyway it's not the Queen's fault she didn't give me a present! How could she? She doesn't even know who I am, you idiot!' Harriet runs off in tears.

It seems unlikely that I will achieve my New Year's Resolution of all thank-you letters despatched by St Valentine's Day.

Spouse comes in and scrutinises me with an expression I have only previously seen him bestow upon cold rice pudding.

'You look tired,' he observes accusingly.

'Of course I'm tired!' A strange yell bursts from my throat. 'If this was a hundred years ago, do you know how many people would be doing my daily work? A cook, a housemaid, a parlourmaid and a nanny. Not to mention the gardener and footman.'

'I don't think many of the middle classes had such extensive establishments.' Spouse awards me his sardonic historian's smile. 'Frankly, as a housewife, you've got delusions of grandeur.'

'And as a husband,' I reply crisply, 'you've got delusions of adequacy.' Stalk out haughtily. Best moment of the year so far.

As it is his turn to look after the kids, I withdraw to my study, where Fanny Hoddle is stalled at appalling moment of crisis in early-twentieth-century mining village.

'What is it, Gertrude?' she stammered. Outside, a factory hooter rose and fell like the wan demented wail of the damned – or so it seemed to Fanny, halfway through Paradise Lost. [Unpleasant thought – did they have factory hooters in early twentieth century? Damn history.] *Gertrude cast her eyes down upon the rag rug.*

'I have been offered a position,' Gertrude murmured, 'in a gentleman's household at Aix-à-Lauvère. M. Boursin is a widower with two daughters, Françoise-Eloise and Violette-Emanuelle.'

How could a mere Fanny compete with such pulchritude of nomenclature? Poor Fanny's knees buckled as her world crumbled. Intellectually, emotionally and spiritually, she was Gertrude's creature.

'Sit down, dear,' murmured Gertrude gently, 'and let me fix you a roll-up. You will get used to the idea very soon, I am sure. Think of the exciting letters I shall be able to send you about la vie en France, as I shall have to start thinking of it.'

'France be buggered!' Fanny burst out, for the first time in her life, into her father's linguistic heritage. 'You can't wait to go, can you? You don't care about me at all! You think you can fob me off wi' a few French letters!'

And she dashed Gertrude's proffered cigarette to the floor and stamped on it with her tight-laced, strict little boots. [Something for everybody in this one.]

Gertrude shrugged, and her clear eyes wandered to the window, staring beyond Berpsover, beyond Boulogne, while Fanny's bosom shook with convulsive sobs. Paradise Lost indeed. Milton did not know the half of it.

'I hope you're writing something really useful,' remarks Spouse, putting his head round the door. 'Where is the Flash?'

'We've run out of Flash,' I inform him. Ah! How true! 'You'll have to use Ecover Floor Soap.'

Spouse groans and withdraws. I try not to speculate about what might have been spilt on the kitchen floor. Turn back to Bonkbuster but seem to have run out of spark as well. I can, however, think of something else I can write which will be just as Really Useful.

Grasping the pen in my left hand, and dribbling and thumbing the page slightly more oft than is my wont, I begin.

Dear Ant Espleth, Thank you very muck for the Fuzy Felts they are ase I pla with them all the tim I hop you ar wel Mumy sends her love love Harriet
OXOXOOOOOXXXXXXX

Wonder why I did not think of this long ago.

6

four

BUY NEW RED PINAFORE dress for Harriet. She has suddenly and violently grown out of all her clothes. I have gradually and gently grown out of all mine, so purchase new black skirt, shorter than is my wont. As soon as we get home, we both eagerly don new togs. Warn Harriet that new clothes stop being exciting after about fifteen minutes.

It soon becomes clear that my black skirt is made from the kind of cloth that attracts, retains and displays every fibre of the material world. It subsequently becomes apparent that Harriet's red pinafore dress is made from the sort of stuff which sheds thousands of small gouts of scarlet fluff over everything it comes into contact with.

Harriet sits on my knee for five minutes and when she gets up, I find I am wearing a scarlet and black mohair skirt. Cannot decide whether this illustrates the importance of the random in the sphere of scientific research, or the futility of shopping for clothes.

Spouse remarks that the old skirt I am wearing is presumably resurrected from the early 1970s, and I should remember that, since then, the quality of my knees has changed. Retire, hurt, into comfortable old tracksuit. Spouse observes that if women who wore tracksuits could see themselves departing, they would have second thoughts. Depart. Have second thoughts about not killing Spouse yet, but am distracted by the phone ringing.

It is Elaine from over the road. She tells me that she has got a new lodger and he is intriguing. Am intrigued. She says he goes to a Turkish bath on Thursdays and has asked her to accompany him but she hasn't got the bottle to go alone so might I like to go too? The thought of warm steam particularly welcome at this time of year, so agree.

'Oh good, but perhaps I ought to warn you that it's naturist,' she adds. Feel, but conceal, qualm. Wonder if Spouse's strictures about departing women in tracksuits also apply to departing women without tracksuits. Can I lose $1\frac{1}{2}$ stone by Thursday? Attempt, without success, to examine backs of knees. Feel dizzy.

Enter sitting room where Spouse is watching *A Question of Sport*. Attempt to engage him in conversation about the

7

weather and wonder, with more desperation than conviction, if February is the start of Spring. Spouse observes only that the nights will soon be drawing in again.

David Coleman, permanently agog as usual, shows us a film of a mêlée in a goalmouth, freezes the frame, and enquires What Happened Next?

Suddenly world goes dark. Assume I have died, and therefore will never know what happened next. Congratulate myself on transcending the material world so painlessly. I appear to be comfortably seated – upon heavenly sofa, perhaps: in some ante-room to Paradise.

'Sod it!' Spouse's aggrieved tones burst rudely through the celestial peace. 'An effing power cut.'

Grope to window and establish that, next door, Bernard and Audrey Twill's lights are still on, so it must be our very own little malfunction and Spouse cannot curse MEB as usual. He curses me instead for not thoughtfully providing torches and candles in every room, and groans at the obligation to exercise his manly duties.

'It must be wonderful being a woman at a time like this,' he remarks. I retort, entirely without conviction, that it is wonderful being a woman at any time.

Recall that Alice gave me scented candles for Christmas, and grope my way towards sideboard. Bark my shins on Harriet's Big Red Fun Bus, but find candles and unwrap in the dark. Alas, Alice did not provide matches so must boldly go to kitchen. Bump into Spouse. He feels strangely alien. A case of *in obscuro veritas*.

Soon a quaint glow spreads through the kitchen, making even the piles of washing-up look picturesque and Renaissance. Spouse examines the fuse box by candlelight and fails to find any fault – a most uncharacteristic lapse on his part. He growls that since modern life utterly dependent on electricity supply, we may as well go to bed as there is nothing else to do.

Remark that candlelight is flattering and that power cuts are oft rumoured to have an effect on the birth-rate. Spouse grunts sardonically and shuffles off upstairs. He is carrying a torch, but not for me. I linger at kitchen table, comforted by the thought that by candlelight my hands look rather like Milton's.

five

For once, the sun shone on Berpsover. Beyond the slag-heaps, over the softly rounded mosses of Allison Dale, the damarts were in bloom. Fanny's little boots scrambled gallantly over stone and scree: higher, higher, she climbed, until her young bosom heaved with the effort of aspiration.

'By 'eck!' she gasped, pausing for breath by a clump of bog asphodel and cowberry. Her fragrant pants wreathed the still-bare branches of a Macclesthorn, at which the tree quivered gently, as if it would fain burst into leaf in response to her ambrosial presence.

Would Gertrude be there? Fanny's green speckled eyes scoured the horizon, but there was no sign of life. She stooped to gather a bouquet for her beloved: Hairy Woodrush, Nipplewort and Fine Bent Grass. A little austere perhaps, but Gertrude would like that. Fanny scrambled onward, and as she rounded the pinnacle of boulders known as Bragg's Tackle, a faint wisp of smoke caught her eye, and she recognised, with a leap of the heart, the scent of Gertrude's favourite tobacco: Hardacre's Thick Old Shag.

Gertrude was seated on a mat of Grimmia Pulvinata gazing thoughtfully out across the glittering sheet of Rough Dike Reservoir.

'Hello, darling,' she murmured vaguely.

'Ey up, tha bonny cossup, here's a nosegay for ee,' cried Fanny. But Gertrude did not seem as enchanted as usual by her friend's lapse into dialect. She sniffed the Nipplewort moodily and tossed it aside on to a late Pliocene rack of shale. Fanny had one of her sudden wild pangs of tempus fugit.

'Eee, where shall thee and me be in't far, far future?' she cried. 'Where shall we be, Gertrude, in 1937, 'appen?'

'I intend to spend my middle years in Paris,' observed Gertrude. Fanny did not like the singular personal pronoun. That I stabbed her like a knife.

'I've had an idea!' she panted. 'I could get a position in France, too! I could also be a governess in a gentleman's house in Aix-à-Lauvère! Perhaps your Monsieur Boursin has a friend who needs such help! We could be together, Gertrude! Ensemble!'

With a final desperate effort Fanny threw an eager arm around Gertrude's shoulder. But her erstwhile inamorata shook it off and stood up.

'I doubt if that would be feasible, my dear,' she sighed. 'But say – shall we not bathe naked in the Rough Dike Reservoir? The weather is so very fine.'

Fanny hesitated, a deep crimson blush mantling her fine cheek. How could she tell Gertrude that her mother had sewn her into her liberty bodice in October, and the stitches were not due to be unpicked until the Macclesthorn was in bloom?

'Mummy! We've found this magazine it's everso funny!'

Reluctantly remove consciousness from Edwardian Berpsover and relocate in *fin-de-siècle* Byelorusbridge. My children, their faces wreathed in ugly sniggers, are waving *Private Eye* at me.

'There's this man he's got a roll of paper coming out of his mouth and it says SHIT SHIT SHIT YOU BASTARD. Hee hee hee!'

'He's receiving a fax from the Devil,' adds Henry helpfully.

Confiscate *Private Eye*.

'Please Mum can we have a fax?'

'No.'

'But can we send away for the Rice Krispies Super Sega Zapper? And enter the competition, please, Mum?'

'Oh, all right.'

Have bought approximately 6 cwt of Rice Krispies recently to make sure of having enough tokens to send away for small deadly device which emits eight different sounds, each one, no doubt, capable of giving a parent a migraine. Fill in form. Competition requires us to invent name for Rice Krispies computer game. Suggest The Rat Rice. Quite struck by my own brilliance.

'Why's that funny?' asks Harriet, annoyed by my self-congratulatory simpering.

Rather perturbed at the thought that tonight I must go to the Turkish bath with Elaine-over-the-road. Oh well. At least it will be warmer than Rough Dike Reservoir.

six

To RUSBRIDGE TURKISH BATHS Naturist Evening. Unwisely inform Spouse of the naked truth at which he utters loud bellow of laughter and declares that menopausal delusion can lead to all sorts of aberrant behaviour. Indignantly insist I am only going as a favour to Elaine-over-the-road as she hasn't enough bottle to go by herself. Do not mention that whole expedition masterminded by her new lodger, as yet unmet by me.

Hasten across road at appointed hour with towel, shampoo, etc, leaving children to be put to bed by Spouse. ('Snot fair! Why can't we come?!') Elaine's lodger is called Fred, has a Cortina and is an upholsterer. He is fiftyish with thick grey hair and shirt unbuttoned to reveal gold-plated razor-blade hanging round his neck. He addresses us as Gews. Find this rather pleasant as have not been a girl for at least ten years, and was a little dashed when last in Italy to discover I had evolved into a Signora.

Arrive at Turkish bath – grimy backstreet area of Rusbridge suggestive of Victorian murder. Fred insists on paying our entry fees. Heart hammers at prospect of undressing in front of elegant youthful types with tans. In the event, however, door to changing room opens to reveal whole families, the middle-aged, the old and the obese cheerfully letting it all hang out. Not so much Le Bain Turc as Hogarth in Undress. Avert my gaze tactfully from all pubic areas and divest myself. Cheered by the fact that I am not the fattest person there by several hundredweight. Elaine displays the streamlined look of the childless.

'Tell me,' she whispers when we are immobilised on adjoining couches in very hot room, 'who was that handsome chap who used to spend a lot of time at your place last year? With the battered old van?'

'Oh,' I murmur casually, emboldened by nudity, 'just my lover.'

Elaine's eyes bulge.

'You *lucky* thing!' she breathes. 'Where did you meet him? I'm desperate for a bit of male company but I simply never meet anybody.'

We look round the room and agree, *sotto voce*, that Fred is the most presentable chap there, neither bald nor stout, and looking quite like Leonard Bernstein now his razor-blade is off.

'The trouble is,' whispers Elaine, 'I really want someone like Kevin Costner and there aren't many about.'

Agree, and lament. We then swim – delicious sensation – and venture into sauna where my brains are boiled. Fred lures the compliant Elaine into the Steam Room and the Icy Plunge Pool but I know my limitations and preserve a medium-rare ambience until it is time to take my new silken skin home. Wonder if next time I should bring the children. Spouse, of course, wouldn't be seen dead nude. Offer him my velvety arm to caress but he begs to be excused as he has a note from his Mum.

Fall into bed and turn to stone for eight hours. Rise refreshed, and after despatching children to school rush to study.

'Come on in, Fanny, it's terribly bracing!' Gertrude waved a freckled arm above the sparkling spume of Rough Dike Reservoir. Fanny hesitated on the brink, goosepimples rippling on her pearly buttocks, her nipples rearing skyward like small pink rockets. It was no use. She must take the plunge – literally, for once. She perched for a moment on tiptoe, then leapt, the summer light flashing on her flanks as on a nubile dolphin.

At the icy embrace of the reservoir she screamed aloud. Then both girls swam, splashed and wrestled, heedless of aught save their youth and strength.

Suddenly Fanny noticed something, and tugged at what would have been Gertrude's sleeve had she been clothed.

'There's somebody up on Gran Tor,' she whispered. 'In the shadow of Bragg's Tackle. Look!'

Gertrude peered into the sun. There was indeed a figure lurking by the pinnacle of rock, gazing intently down upon the girls.

'It reminds me of that bit from the Faerie Queene,*' said Gertrude, ' "Two naked Damzelles he therein espied, Which therein bathing, seemed to contend, And wrestle wantonly . . ." '*

Fanny sighed. She would never be as learned as Gertrude. And as she gazed upward at the furtive spectator, she felt that her Eden had been intruded on by a serpentine presence. Her ripped liberty bodice lay on a nearby rock. How, with modesty, could she ever regain it?

If publisher not ravished by the above, I give up.

seven

Gertrude stood up, waist deep in Rough Dike Reservoir, and shouted a ringing challenge to the distant figure skulking in the shadow of the Tor.

'Come down if you dare!' she cried. 'Face us if you're man enough – if not, begone!'

The figure hesitated, then began to scramble down the scree towards them. Fanny instinctively ducked below the water, preserving her maiden modesty up to her chin. Gertrude, however, faced him, indignant and brazen, her arms folded commandingly across her regal bosom.

Eventually he stumbled to a halt at the waterside, his face as scarlet as a cock's comb, his glasses misted up with exertion.

'Forgive me, ladies! I intended no intrusion.' The voice was cultured and gentle. 'Allow me to introduce myself. My name is Melvyn Potter, and I am an artist in oils, chalks and watercolours. I was sketching some mosses when your laughter attracted my attention, and the enchanting tableau you presented reminded me of Giovanni Lamborghini's The Naiads. *I don't suppose you would consider posing for me – either here, in the bos . . . er of nature, or in my little studio in Hawkspitdale?'*

For an instant Fanny was almost charmed by the thought of the little studio, but Gertrude seized the initiative.

'We are not deluded, Mr Potter, by your specious apologias!' she announced. 'We recognise lubricious intent, however it is cloaked in aesthetic aspiration. Stuff your studio!' And she dived for an instant beneath the waves, emerged with a handful of mud, and hurled it at the hapless Mr Potter, badly spattering his Fair Isle pullover. Fanny could not help feeling that Mr Potter did not entirely deserve Gertrude's onslaught. But she remained silent and submerged.

Horrified to discover it is already 3 p.m. Dive into car but, halfway to school, become aware of intestinal malaise. Sweat breaks out between shoulder-blades, ears flutter, etc, and am forced to park illegally by War Memorial and rush into public loo. Why is it that loos are always being cleaned at such moments? And why, in the one place where deafening muzak desirable, is one faced with sepulchral silence? Cough loudly, and hum unconvincingly, to hide distress.

Pick up children, and inform them plaintively I am ill, without effect. They insist on demanding Monster Munches and Fizzy Dippers, at the mention of which my pancreas ceases to be stationary. Steer conversation away towards children's TV but gorge also rises at thought of Turtles, Sesame Street, and of course Muffin the Mule.

On arrival home, consult *Family Health Encyclopaedia* and decide I am suffering from Salmonella, Beri Beri and Clostridium Perfringens – unless the latter a refugee from herbaceous border. Momentarily distracted by diagram showing life-cycle of the hookworm, a tropical parasite 'which uses its sharp curved tooth-like structures to cling to the bowel'. Vow never to stray south of Wantage. Description of hookworm reminds me somehow of predatory fringe of gutter press. Always so obsessed with sexual secrets. Must avoid high-minded hypocrisy, however, as I am, after all, engaged in producing tawdry bonkbuster appealing to similar instincts.

Bitterly regret telling Elaine-over-the-road that I have had a lover. Certain this information will somehow spill out all over Spouse – or worse, children: real victims of adulterous passion. Shed a tear. Within minutes, however, they have charged in from the garden and spread mud through recently vacuumed house. Tears dry up nicely, and bile ducts brim anew. (Mem.: when next buying wall-to-wall carpet, choose one the colour of mud, not wretched oatmeal.)

Attempt to distract myself from stomach bug by reading cricketing press, but am moved to nausea by repeated mentions of Lamb, Stewart, Brotham, Ambrose and S'ua.

Spouse returns in state of self-pitying fatigue from healthy day's work, wolfs down huge cheese sandwich and demands to know why I'm looking unusually grim. Inform him that, like Yeats, I feel I am fastened to a dying animal.

'Well,' sighs Spouse, 'I just hope it's housetrained.'

eight

HARRIET WILL BE SEVEN next week, so I must toe the Party line. 'I don't want a conjuror!' she roars before one is even offered. Experience similar feelings at approach of Budget. 'They always do the same tricks! I want boys!' Tempted to warn her that boys always do the same tricks, too, but refrain. Let her discover it all by herself.

'Gabrielle had a pirate party and Emily had a witches party! I want a wild animals party!'

Observe that if she insists on inviting boys, that is what she will get, but finally concede that wildlife theme may be indicated by a few marzipan hyenas on cake.

Elaine-over-the-road drops in to ask my advice: should she accept her lodger's invitation out to dinner? Not sure. Warn that evening may take on a wild animals theme. Elaine undeterred. She turns the conversation around once more to my chequered past, and asks me what was Tom's worst quality. Reply that he had no carapace. Add sardonically that Spouse's worst quality is that he has nothing else.

Elaine hesitates for a few seconds, then asks me what is a carapace. Have often thought my life would have been a lot more idyllic had I had a larger bosom and smaller vocabulary. Elaine remarks that I look tired. Perhaps she is not going to be a bosom chum after all. Confide party anxieties. She sympathises, but it is the bloodless sympathy of the childless.

Next day I drive into Rusbridge and order cake from new twee baker's called Crumbs. Tempted to request marzipan axolotls, but sense further vocabulary trouble, and confine request to snails. Dash home again, desperate to complete my daily dose of Bonkbuster before further party duties intrude.

'Fanny,' murmured Gertrude, the goosepimples galloping across her pert shoulder-blades, 'pat me dry, will you, darling?'

But Fanny hesitated . . .

Doorbell rings. Fanny will have to hesitate for longer than she thinks. It is Elaine-over-the-road. Am beginning to think she is not over-the-road nearly enough. But this uncharitable thought dispelled by her presenting me with large book entitled *Jane Asher's Children's Parties*.

'I was just browsing in the bookshop,' said Elaine, 'and there it was, and I instantly thought of you.'

Express gratitude, though secretly marvel at lifestyle which could include browsing in bookshop on a Thursday morning.

Peruse Jane Asher, boggle at artistic panache of Pirate Cake, Crown Cake, Disco Cake, etc, and quickly become convinced that Asher is reincarnation of Benvenuto Cellini, who, I seem to recall, started life as a confectioner of some sort. Feel deeply inadequate. Have only attempted to bake a cake once and could not get it up.

Book suggests some wonderful games, including one called The Naughty Letter which should equip children for eventual career in gutter journalism.

Mrs Body, faithful cleaner, volunteers to do catering. Accept with gratitude, and decide Jane Asher's Red Setter-shaped sandwiches and stylish silver sweets ('available from good confectioners') will have to wait till next year.

Had rashly promised to take Harriet to the local Toys'Я'Us (or Toys'Я'Usbridge as we think of it). Had even more rashly promised to buy her Little Miss Magic Hair, a doll whose hair turns white when stroked with heated (or is it iced?) hairbrush. Feel smug, since my hair turns white all by itself without having to be stroked at all.

On the way to Toys'Я'Usbridge, my venerable Volvo is sexually harassed by usual vile fat man in transit van. Can feel sixteen more hairs turning white. Recall was overtaken once by child cyclist, but it was in Portugal.

In the south transept of Toys'Я'Usbridge, we bump into Charlotte, middle-class Mum of Jocasta, one of Harriet's schoolmates. Charlotte blushes and stammers that they were destined for Early Learning Centre but Jocasta insisted. Harriet recklessly invites Jocasta to her party even though she knows there are already too many. Jocasta joyfully accepts.

Birthday and party now only hours away, but I must face it like a man. Although facing it like a man would mean ignoring it altogether.

nine

HARRIET'S PARTY EXPLODES UPON my head. Have hired church hall to avoid wear and tear on own home. Six small boys arrive and begin sliding about and fighting. Request that they desist. Request ignored. Repeat request loudly. Sliding and fighting increase, accompanied by banshee yells. Open mouth wide as Fingal's Cave and utter The Perfect Hostess's Polite Scream for order. Mayhem continues.

Spouse enters bearing cake and looking martyred. Mildly he asks boys to calm down. Instant peace. Male conspiracy of mutual respect. I am, of course, Only A Mum. Experience, but mercifully overcome, brief Herodian impulse.

Little girls are sitting in a clump discussing frills. Gabrielle has a pair of shoes with a tiny caged bird set into the sole, in a prism of perspex. This seems a rather metaphysical conceit somehow. If William Blake were here, no doubt he would write a poem about it.

> A robin redbreast in a shoe
> Puts all heaven in a stew . . .

Wish Wm Blake was here, especially in absence of entertainer. Perhaps he could conjure up a few angels. Preferably evicting angels with swords. They'd have to be male, though, or their allcluias would fall on deaf ears.

By 6 p.m. floor of church hall resembles giant pizza. But, alleluia, tea is consumed, games concluded with acrimonious debate, lavatories devastated, and Harriet's heart broken because Wayne has made it clear he prefers Gabrielle. The Party's over.

Mums arrive to collect. Spouse emerges refreshed from sports pages of paper he has furtively hidden behind for most of the time. He exudes charm and looks distinguished (i.e. the male version of old). One or two mums seem to imply that I am lucky to have a husband willing and able to attend children's party. They do not, however, suggest to Spouse that he is lucky to have a wife willing to organise and orchestrate the whole débâcle, and refrain from rebuking him for reading a newspaper throughout.

Show teeth in approximation to smile, and distribute party bags. Jason instantly complains that he hasn't got a Monster in his Pocket like all the other boys. Recognise castration anxiety and slip him an extra Smartie.

On the way home, Harriet observes that she feels really sorry for boys having to do all that rough stuff. Then she falls

to singing a song entitled 'I'm Too Sexy For My Shirt . . .'
Alas, I fear the days of Goosey Gander are behind us.

'Outrageous!' sniffed Gertrude as they strode womanfully across
the burgeoning tufts of Heath Wort. Ahead of them, a pair of moor tits
flickered among the thistles. But the sun had gone in.

'Perhaps he meant well,' murmured Fanny. Something about
Melvyn Potter had appealed to her. His faintly metropolitan accent,
perhaps: the stains of Crimson Lake on his fingertips; the exciting
whiff of turpentine. She privately resolved to walk to Hawkspitdale
the next Lord's Day, and lounge picturesquely by the canal – just in
case Fate intended them to meet again.

'Artists are all very well, my dear,' commented Gertrude, 'as long
as they are French, or Italian. What does this Melvyn Potter know of
darkness, passion, heat? Englishmen make hopeless artists and worse
lovers. Remember that!'

'What about Scots?' faltered Fanny. She had admired a lithograph
of the rugged crags of Ben Eltoun and thought that any sensibility
nourished in its shade must possess a profound romanti–

'Scots!' cried Gertrude. A peal of contemptuous laughter burst from
her perfect lips. 'Show me a Scotsman with a soul! No, Fanny: they
are all rigour and economy and nasty white knees. What do they know
of the deep thrilling groundswell of the Masculine?'

Fanny could not hazard a guess. Gertrude gathered herself a hazel
twig from the hedge, and set forth whistling a love-song from the
Auvergne, and slashing at thistles as she went.

'When are you departing for Aix-à-Lauvère?' Fanny enquired
lightly, though her heart smote her at the sad discovery that, for her,
Gertrude's departure could not come soon enough.

Fridge empty, so Spouse boldly goes to take-away. Aren't I
lucky?

ten

'Ma chère Fanny. Well! Here I am in Aix-à-Lauvère, all
dancing light and avenues of plane trees. A more elegant
establishment than M. Boursin's could not be imagined. An
eighteenth-century façade, harmonious and yet exotic, with

shutters, veranda, pots of geraniums, etc. I sit in the fragrant shade of a great cedar, feast upon fresh figs and sip my Château de Renault . . .'

Fanny groaned, screwed up the paper and hurled it on to the fire. She could not bear to think of Gertrude sipping her Château in all that dancing light. Suddenly she hated Berpsover. She leapt up, ran to the window, and glared out through the drizzle at the gasworks, the slag-heaps, and the miserable hunched roof of the Antipathitarian Chapel. Was this the only vista that life had to offer her eager young orbs? Crystalline tears burst from them at the thought.

Dashing them away, she seized the local organ – The Berpsover Bugle. *As usual, it was all steam-hammers and industrial mutilations, second-hand clogs and choir practices. She ignored the advertisements ('Uncle Joe's Mint Balls Keep You All Aglow') and leafed her way to the last page, below the obituaries. And what she saw there made her heart leap and her scalp creep.*

'Assistant Mistress required for Board School at Auchtereekie, West Lothian. Apply, with details of experience and the names of two referees, to The Proctor, Hector K. McGillicuddy, The Manse, Auchtereekie.'

Suddenly Fanny smelt heather and seemed to see eagles wheeling in the azure vault of heaven. Freedom! Hope kindled in her breast.

Am bored to death with breasts, but soldier on. Oh, for a nice quiet little job in Woolworth's. Extraordinarily laborious, the process of getting Fanny to Auchtereekie in order for her to be fascinated by various members of the Shadow Cabinet in Caledonian attire.

'Mummee! My wobbly tooth *still* hasn't come out! Gabrielle's got four out and she's only six!'

Harriet wails disconsolately. I can imagine her in four years' time, impatient for a bosom. At least one can buy pre-pubescent bras. In fact, these days one can buy bras for six-year-olds. Sawn-off vests, exposing to the cruel March winds the tender infantile kidney, whilst draping in false modesty what does not yet exist.

Why stop at six? Why not bikinis and high heels for the newborn? Make them aware of their glorious destiny. If only I had the entrepreneurial spirit I would instantly launch a range of sexy togs for kids: Bimbino, perhaps.

Elaine-over-the-road rings to ask if I will accompany her to Callanetics, an exercise plan suitable, she swears, for the Older Buttock. Decline, with synthetic regret, inventing hamstring injury.

Spouse appears, yawns, stretches, and makes the faint cracking noise with his jaw which has always irritated me, even when I was madly in love with him back in 1492. He looks more than usually lugubrious and self-pitying.

'I think I'm going down with something,' he reports tragically. 'I know I promised to take them to the cinema this afternoon but I'm afraid I shall have to go to bed.'

He withdraws, with a long-drawn-out melancholy sigh, rather like the North Sea on a quiet day in Dunwich.

So it seems that Fanny, destined to arrive in Auchtereekie this afternoon, will be unavoidably delayed in Berpsover. Wonder if I have been a little too harsh on her. Perhaps I shall give Gertrude food-poisoning. Too many truffles and fartichokes in the shade of the cedar tree. Serve her right.

'We can still go to *Honey, I Shrunk the Kids*, can't we, Mum?' enquires Harriet anxiously. 'Or I don't mind not going to that, as long as I can have extra pocket money and have my ears pierced.'

'You can do no such thing! It looks awful on little girls! You'll have to wait till you're sixteen.'

'Gabrielle's had her ears pierced.'

'Sod Gabrielle!'

'Don't swear. I'm a Brownie!'

Sod Gabrielle possibly also blasphemous. Hope so, anyway.

eleven

ILLNESS HAS CHANGED SINCE I was young: from Virol to viral. Whole family felled by flu: Harriet and Spouse histrionically, Henry hideously, self selflessly.

'I wish I'd never beed bord!' howls Harriet, festering in a nest of disintegrating Teddies. Minutes later, however, she is well enough to sneak to bathroom and hold thermometer under hot tap in order to give me momentary heart failure.

'I'm afraid some snot has got into the Walkman, Mummy,' laments Henry. Could be worse. *Sic transistor gloria mundi.*

Spouse struggles unsuccessfully to overcome his deep jealousy of Simon Schama's TV programmes about Rembrandt.

'If you turned the sound down,' he comments sourly, 'he looked like a manic gecko.'

Forbear to observe that Spouse looks like a dead crocodile even with the sound turned up.

Spouse is pronounced fit enough to watch *A Question of Sport*. Hope David Coleman's voice will break soon. Spouse shows uncanny ability to identify jockeys by their eyebrows. Doubt if this gift will lead to international recognition equivalent to that enjoyed by Simon Schama, however.

Go to bed hoping for dream about manic gecko, but am surprised or rather – and this is the odd thing about dreams – am *not* surprised to find myself in crowded ante-room with John Major, who is being pestered by hostile journalists. If only he had remained Major-Ball he could have let 'em have it with both barrels. His biggest mistake was to drop his Ball. Crowds depart, Major fixes me with torrid stare, his glasses steam up, he seizes my hand, suddenly gasps, 'Dulcie – I wunt you!' and falls punting on my breast.

Awake with violent twitch of limbs to find Spouse groping the bedside cupboard – the only thing he does grope, these days. Perhaps he has celebrated a decade of market forces by privatising his privates.

'Where's the Vick?'

O Spouse, thou art sick. Find what proves to be the Old Vick but Spouse irritably insists he means Sinex. The folly of new names. I want my Montgomeryshire back.

Spouse syringes both nostrils with ghastly ripping sound he would never have dreamed of emitting in the early days when he was first trying to impress me. Confide details of dream.

'Any woman of spirit would be dreaming about Paddy Ashdown,' Spouse rebukes me, and falls asleep, presumably in search of Hillary Clinton. All this electoral soliciting has penetrated nation's subconscious.

The PM was appreciative of me in my dream. He is remarkably loyal to the idea of the Broadly Flat – amongst whom I fear I must be numbered. He also seems embarrassed by the whole thing, as any decent human being should be. But oh, the burdens of democracy! Especially when the body politic, as well as the body of the voter, is taxed by inflammation and inflamed by taxation.

What a burden the High Life must be to politicians of modest origin.

'Tha'll come to no good, wi' thi education and thi hoity-toity ways!' roared Fanny's father from his fireside chair. Her mother pressed a bundle into her hand, wrapped in stained paper.

''Tis a morsel o'black pudden,' she whispered. 'Tha mustn't lose tha bonny looks, ma lass!' And a tear fled down her crumpled cheek.

'I'll write, mother,' whispered Fanny, kissing her. She picked up her modest case, and walked out into the sulphurous rain of Berpsover.

Wish I could vote for Dennis Skinner. But, alas, I live in Wilts. Indeed, most of the time I wilts in Wilts.

Harriet still too ill for school, so watch *Sesame Street* with her. Had forgotten how wonderful it was: total joy and miracle. For a precious few minutes the election campaign is forgotten. Though the Cookie Monster does bear a striking resemblance to Chris Patten.

twelve

So this is it, thought Fanny, as with a plangent exhalation of steam, the Great Northern Locomotive Auld Crankie drew into the station at The Creels o'Faucht. A bobbing lantern seemed to beckon her through the ebony night. The School Board of Auchtereekie had arranged for her to be met and conveyed to a Mrs Salmond's where she was to lodge.

Auld Crankie departed, with a series of deep chuffs reminiscent of Fanny's father after his morning pipe of Hardacre's Thick Old Shag. Through the whirling miasma of smoke and smuts, Fanny caught sight of a sour-faced man with a thin red beard. He nodded. 'Mess Hoddle?'

Fanny supposed she was. So, coming to Scotland had transformed her from a Miss to a Mess. How symbolic, she thought, those two bleak monosyllables, of women's lot.

'*I'm tae convey ye to Mestress Salmond's.*'

He took her bag, escorted her to a high trap, and offered her a tartan rug beneath which Fanny cowered as, with a jerk, they set off through the night.

They soon left The Creels o'Faucht, and drove through deep countryside. Fanny did not fear for her maiden honour, however, for inside her whippetskin muff she clutched the silver and gallstone hatpin which had been Gertrude's parting gift.

'*Are there hills hereabouts?*' *she enquired, in jostled bursts, as the extent of their journey seemed to require social discourse.*

'*Yon's the Braes o'Sloggie,*' *muttered her companion with a jerk of the head.* '*And yon's Benn Toonie, and yon's th' Brig o'Deer Whiskerrie.*'

The cart leapt over a little humpbacked bridge. Fanny's hatpin intruded itself brusquely into her stays, and became entangled therein.

'*Yon's Garrie Hart Burn,*' *her guide continued,* '*that flows intae Loch Bogie. And yon,*' *– a final, conclusive jerk of the head –* '*are the Falls of Dan Drough.*'

'*How very interesting,*' *said Fanny politely.* '*Thank you so much.*'

Though it would have been a lot more interesting, of course, if one could actually have seen any of it.

The sun comes out with unnecessary vehemence as usual at this time of year, revealing grubby wallpaper, films o'filth on the windowpanes, and the inescapable fact that Time hath digged deep trenches in my brow and then gone off for a tea-break leaving a right mess, rather in the manner of British Telecom.

'Mummy,' Harriet eyes me awkwardly, 'please can you wear gloves when you collect me from school because I don't want people to see your Old Hands.'

Inspect hands. They resemble Ordnance Survey map of North Wales: all brown spots, contour lines and wriggly blue rivers.

'Certainly,' I concede, 'as long as you promise always to wear sunglasses and Factor 20 suncream when you go out to play.'

'Bo-RING!' snaps my child.

Any grandchildren will presumably have to wear goggles and gas-masks if our factories go on making Porsches, Sindies and Double Whammy Death Ray Guns, but our standard of living will have been preserved and that's the vital thing, isn't it? Cannot imagine life without a new car every year and 1700 varieties of biscuits in Tesco's – indeed without these modern conveniences life would be hollow and meaningless.

A blackbird sings bravely in the dusk. Tears burst from ducts. Fear that Spring has well and truly broken. Confide my thoughts about western industrial society to Spouse who cries, 'Oh why don't you join the bloody Green Party and have done with it?'

Or perhaps I should throw in my ancient Celtic hand with the Welsh Nats?

Feel guilty. Still do not know the meaning of Karaoke and fear it is too late to ask without calling down ridicule upon my head. Thought at first it was a Sumo wrestler, Caribbean cocktail or new breakfast cereal. Still in the dark. Will have to ask Henry. Strange how quickly one's children become the Old Hands in this Brave New World.

thirteen

TERRIFIC DREAM IN WHICH John Smith enfolds me in cracking embrace. Awake and for several minutes recollect with admiration his Caledonian *gravitas*, the large imperturbable lips, etc. Why had I never before noticed the erotic potential of this ensemble? Why had I been mesmerised by Gordon Brown's pallor, brilliance and dark Heathcliffian locks? Must the Gothic always triumph over the Classical? Oh fie.

Alice rings from New Orleans to wish me a Happy Easter and impertinently enquires how is my love life. Inform her that it revolves around dreams of politicians.

'Oh, Dulcie!' she cries in disgust. 'Not Ian Paisley again!' Hastily change subject. What a memory she has.

'What's happening in *The Archers*?' she enquires. 'Are they still being all modern and depraved?'

Assure her that Eddie and Nelson have Come Out, Mike Tucker has run amok with a Kalashnikov, and Peggy Archer has taken to Primal Scream. Alice reminds me how lucky I am to be within earshot of this epic. She and Saskia are contemplating further travels in Central and South America.

'We're torn,' she confesses, 'between Zihuatanejo and Machu Picchu.' Recall similar feelings once, long ago, on cycling holiday, *vis-à-vis* Beccles and Bungay.

'Ah well, throw yourself into your work,' recommends Alice. Ha! The only stimulating thing she has thrown herself into recently is a Jacuzzi.

Spouse puts his head round door and ignores the fact that I am on the phone.

'I've got cramp in my extremities,' he reports sombrely. 'I've looked it up in *The BMA Book of How to be Ill* and I think it's Motor Neurone Disease.'

Convey this info to Alice, who says she remembers me telling her long ago that his Big End had gone.

Conversation concluded, on her part with specious sympathy and on mine, with murderous envy. Why should Alice have all the Machu Picchu? Ah well. Pick up pen and urge imagination towards inner landscape.

My dearest Gertrude,
I write from Mrs Salmond's small cottage, a granite hut which crouches under the shrieking wind from the north-east, in a remote corner of Auchtereekie. My room is of modest size – indeed, I can blow out my candle, lock the door, open the window and empty the chamberpot without having to leave my bed – but I am comfortable here. The absence of a reproving paternal presence is a blessing. [Hope Alice and Saskia notice that swingeing attack on the patriarchy.]

Mrs Salmond herself is a dear good creature, though I cannot understand a word she says. I'll swear, this morning, she offered me 'Wharrascorragh ock puits a dougie' for breakfast. I suppose you are encountering similar problems in Aix-à-Lauvère. Though your French was always very deft. You are also no doubt spared my meteorological tribulations. (At each gust of wind, my counterpane – a Black Watch tartan adorned with strange poignant stains – capers in the breeze.)

Tomorrow I am to present myself at the school, and meet the headmaster Mr Hector Macrae. I tremble at the thought. What will he be like . . .?

Fanny hesitated before the heavy door, and timidly tapped. She was expecting an authoritarian roar, but the voice which summoned her was light and musical. She entered – and saw Mr Macrae seated in a sunbeam, rather like a Dutch painting of St Jerome in his study, without the beards and lions. Mr Macrae rose, extended a warm and steady hand, and behind his austere eyeglasses there was a twinkling gaze which she found encouraging. Small motes of dust danced above his gleaming pate.

His dignity impressed her. She had seen a bust of Tacitus, once, and fancied that Mr Macrae resembled it. Or was it Cicero? How odd. How unexpected. And yet, of course, Scotland had blossomed during the Enlightenment. Perhaps she too would blossom, or be enlightened here, despite the capering counterpane and the granite. She hoped so.

Aware that sex-and-violence content likely to plummet in the face of all this classical *gravitas*. Suspect shall have to resort to more Gothic all too soon. Spend $1\frac{1}{2}$ minutes imagining enlightened weekend with John Smith in Brighton, but baffled by need to invent plausible alias for hotel register.

fourteen

BONKBUSTER IS STALLED. CANNOT decide which early-twentieth-century Scotsman to launch my heroine at: head-master? Pastor? Procurator Fiscal or indeed Fingal? Tam O'Shanter? Kilted ghillie in vest tossing his caber in morose glen? Wonder if it was true what they said about Queen Victoria and John Brown – a man who, had he lived now, would certainly be in the Shadow Cabinet. Feel over-whelming urge to escape from porridge advertisement.

Rush to bathroom. Reflect that since it is April I should be in Paris. Or Eurodisney as it is now known. Ah well. At least spared French plumbing. Recall, with shudder, Alice and Saskia's old flat in the Latin Quarter where loo was located in evil-smelling cupboard and flush was so inefficient, one could have spat to greater effect. Pull chain with terrific, satisfying, British cascade.

Linger and polish taps: always a sign of desperation. Decide it is time for shadow bathroom cabinet reshuffle. Find huge array of half-finished bottles of Body Shop stuff. Spouse comes in, urinates (unnecessarily loudly, I always feel) and then examines unguents.

'Grapefruit shampoo . . . banana hair putty . . . tangerine oil . . .' he muses. 'Relentlessly vegetarian. If they really want to get a man going they should try liver-and-bacon shampoo. Or salami lip-gloss.'

Inform him indignantly that the purpose of cosmetics is not to get men going. Though privately recall the urgency with which I plastered myself in cucumber-and-tarragon skin milk back in the good old days when I was Tom's dish. But as for Spouse . . .

'I doubt if it would get you going,' I observe with asperity, 'even if I was coated with egg and breadcrumbs and deep-fried.'

Spouse concedes that, were he to take to the cannibalism which is apparently so chic these days, he would prefer something more tender and organic.

He departs, leaving me to eat my heart out.

Why can I not bring myself to discard half-finished bottles of hand-lotion even if it has gone slightly pongy? 'Can always oil the hinges with it,' I think. 'Or clean Harriet's patent leather shoes . . .' Experience similar tender feelings towards veg in bottom of fridge, long after veg has ceased to exhibit any tenderness towards me.

Descend to kitchen and remove from fridge two and a half mouldy swedes. Hesitate.

'Harriet . . . would you like to make some sculptures out of these?'

'Oh yes Mum ace brilliant!'

'No – wait! You might cut yourself.'

Howl of outrage from daughter that I should have offered beguiling opportunity for veg arts and then instantly changed mind.

'I don't care if I do bloody cut myself!'

'And if you do,' adds Henry, 'we can write a letter in blood. That would be cool.'

Forbid further discussion of subject and evict children into garden where they seize old bamboo canes and attempt to eviscerate each other therewith.

Stare balefully at two and a half mouldy swedes. Hastily banish rogue impulse to attempt cuisine with them. Throw in bin. Feel guilty, retrieve and throw in compost bucket.

Troubled by conviction that they will take thirty years to biodegrade in their present cannonball form. Retrieve, grasp knife and try to cut them into small pieces. Knife slips and almost removes left thumb. Blood everywhere. Hold thumb under tap. Water turns to claret. Feel faint and wish I were a vegetable.

Wrap thumb in teatowel, then remember that average used teatowel contains 2000 microbes, many of them deadly. Wrap in clean teatowel. Spouse enters and enquires what's for lunch. Announce I am retiring hurt and it's up to him. Retire to study and approach word-processor single-handed.

Fanny's mouth watered at the smell of Mrs Salmond's neeps and tatties. It had been a busy day: preparing her classroom for the morrow.

'Neeps and tatties,' announced Mrs Salmond. 'We'll soon hae ye sonsie and bonny, ye puir wee killie-croatie.'

Fanny knew that root vegetables produce wind, but she fell to with a will.

Spouse prepares purée of swede: gorge thereon: next morning, whilst in library queue, am seized by severe attack of stand-up colic.

fifteen

ALL THE WAY HOME from Tesco's, Spouse listens to Beethoven's Late Quartets – an infallible sign of deepening hypochondria. Children complain.

'Why can't we have Michael Jackson? Snot fair!'

On arrival, Spouse announces that he is going on a liquid diet. In the past this has meant Old Bushmills, but now he apparently requires soup. Unfortunate that he did not say anything about liquid diet whilst we were actually in Tesco's, and I was loading up with solidities.

Find old tin of Heinz Tomato Soup at the back of the cupboard, and fight off haunting memories of 1950s childhood. Tinned soup, coal fires, *Daily Mirror* with Garth and Jane providing role models. I easily mastered Jane's knack of catching my clothing on door handles, but not to same picturesque effect.

Soup boils. Rescue it guiltily as know Boiling Will Impair the Flavour. Spouse enters, sips and winces.

'Can't bear this tinned stuff. You can taste the tin.' He wanders off burping morosely.

Leaving him safe in the relentless grip of the medical encyclopaedia, and Henry and Harriet engrossed by the spectacle of something televisual called *Top Banana*, I speed back to Tesco's. Still half-distracted by memories of pre-Tesco era with Animal, Vegetable and Mineral and Dan Dare on the wireless.

In remote corner of Tesco's, locate refined soups (e.g. Stilton and broccoli) encased in fragrant cardboard. They look beguilingly like pints of milk. Select several as sure they will appeal to Spouse.

Return to find him ransacking bathroom cabinet in search of Rennie's Rap-Eze – new, delicious indigestion tablets. (How very different from dear old 1950s Milk of Magnesia.)

'It's definitely a peptic ulcer,' he reports gravely. 'Or Van Halsingborg's Syndrome.'

'Ah well,' I soothe, 'there's some really nice soup downstairs – not tinned, either.'

'I don't really fancy soup any more,' sighs Spouse. 'I think I could manage a cup of tea, though.'

Grind teeth, descend and put kettle on. Struggle to open carton of milk, resorting to carving fork and fruit knife and attempting to banish haunting memories of 1950s school-milk bottles with sensible cardboard tops, easily penetrated by any passing tit. Eventually carton is opened, but when I try to pour out milk it spurts forth from three ragged spouts: one on to the table, one into the sugar bowl and one on to my foot. Experience white-hot rage and curse the illusion of progress.

Children run in with toad they have found in garden and ask what would be a toadlike name. Spouse immediately answers 'Norman Stone'.

When children are in bed, Spouse appears with brown paper bag, looks sheepish and says, 'I bought a video the other day.'

Boggle, and brace myself for the sins of the flesh. Spouse produces *The Silence of the Lambs*. Wonder if this is wise, but at least we have the latest in state-of-the-art dyspepsia tablets.

Wonder why Spouse so attracted by the repellent, but suppose he hopes to augment his reserves of menace by picking up a few tips from Anthony Hopkins. Film, though grisly, strangely compelling, though am forced to watch it with my eyes closed much of the time. Cast the occasional glance at Spouse who has gone slightly green.

After the Hopkins character has escaped, leaving a trail of disembowelled and half-ingested guards, Spouse gets up, announces magnanimously that he will get me a cup of tea, and *leaves me alone*. Cringe behind cushions, convinced that Jodie Foster's bowels cannot remain decently hidden much longer. Suspect Spouse's offer to make tea merely a chicken-hearted escape, and wish I had thought of it myself.

Reflect sadly that a society without taboos offers no toe-hold to the artist. Pleased with this thought and wish I were on a TV discussion so people could admire me saying it. Something terrifying appears on TV screen again so close eyes and think of the 1950s. A stealthy tread – my skin creeps, but 'tis Spouse with tray. Apparently he mistook carton of Stilton and broccoli soup for milk carton, so if tea tastes queer it is not altogether Anthony Hopkins's fault.

sixteen

'THE SYMPTOMS OF STOMACH cancer are often mistaken for indigestion,' pronounces Spouse from behind a newspaper, then burps significantly. Forbear to point out that in the past hour he has put away steak, sauté potatoes, broccoli, salad, apricot pie and yogurt, and that if he is suffering from a terminal intestinal condition this is pretty good going. 'I think I shall have to see a specialist,' he sighs, folding up paper and staring morosely into garden, where children are tormenting Norman Stone, their pet toad.

Am no stranger to hypochondria myself: perhaps this is why I find Spouse's so irritating. There is only room for one hypochondriac in any marriage. It is a condition particularly unbecoming to the male sex, somehow, who should banish any hint of weakness and regain bulging biceps and bounding *bonhomie* with a single tin of spinach – preferably unopened.

'Yes, why don't you? I'm sure it'd be reassuring.' Smile brightly and, I hope, not too synthetically.

'And if reassurance is not available, then at least one can make the necessary arrangements.' His turn to attempt smile, without success. 'Changing the will, and so on. Impoverishing the wife and children in favour of the Distressed ex-Gerbils' Sunset Home of East Sussex.'

Try to banish all thoughts of gerbil from my mind. Toad a distinct improvement as children's pet. Exhibits very little emotion. Cannot watch rodentine frenzy for long without urgent desire to ring Amnesty International. All the same – open french windows and bawl, 'Put it down – and Harriet, take those Sindy clothes off it!'

'It's not an IT!' screams Harriet indignantly. 'He's Norman!'

Spouse goes up to bathroom, where he spends increasing amounts of time, these days. Caught him in there yesterday trying to look up his own arse with my powder compact.

'Any mongrel in the street can bite its own arse with ease,' he complained savagely. But then, Spouse has always been rather hard on the human condition.

Myself, am beginning to wonder about God. All those Bible readings on the radio by good actors instead of feeble curates have reminded me what ripping yarns are offered by the Testaments. Am still several light years away from being born again, however. Try to imagine what Jesus would have been like if alive today, but get no further than a vague conviction that he would make a scene in the Reference Library. One of the things I like about him is that he is so often rude.

Spouse unable to mow lawn owing to stomach cramps, and is forced to lie on sofa and watch sporting events on TV. Children request outing. Negotiate hard bargain involving ice creams on the common at 5 p.m. if I am allowed an hour of working solitude first, and they are Not to Disturb Daddy who is Feeling Ill. Feel a certain triumph, as I say this, that I am myself reasonably well. Perhaps there is room in a marriage for two hypochondriacs, after all.

'Miss Hoddle – I would like a word with you after school today if it is not inconvenient. Hector Macrae.'

His handwriting was attractive, thought Fanny, if a little small. It sloped to the right. It had energy. There were no affected curlicues, as adorned Gertrude's envelopes from Aix-à-Lauvère.

The small child who had brought the note wiped his nose upon a ragged sleeve. Snotty noses were a law of Nature at Auchtereekie Board School: inevitable as the purple smoke of heather upon the Braes O'Sloggie.

'My dear Miss Hoddle . . .' Mr Macrae steepled his fingers and inserted them beneath his chin. Fanny's heart missed a beat. My dear – did he mean anything by that? Fanny had heard that the headmaster was a widower. His wife Fiona had been tragically drowned in the Dee whilst trying to bandage the fin of a wounded salmon, seven years ago – long enough, Fanny hoped, for the hurt to heal. Of Mr Macrae, that is, not the salmon. She hoped that she hoped this unselfishly, but time would tell. 'I feel I must warn you,' his clear light eyes played reflectively over her face, 'about the Pastor. Have you met him yet?' Fanny shook her head. 'His name,' said Mr Macrae, with a curious hint of a shudder, 'is MacPravity.' Fanny was intrigued.

Spouse joins trip to common for ice-cream, consumes an entire Choc'n'Mint Intergalactic Fizzy Beastie Feastie, and declares himself seriously ill.

seventeen

TRIP TO MANCHESTER TO give talk on 'Children's Fiction' at bookshop run by Spouse's cousin Charlotte – in which the 'C' is silent. Her famous inefficiency more than compensated for by her gleaming thighs. I welcome twenty-four hours away from domestic duties – most arduous of which is sustained sympathy for Spouse's rampant hypochondria.

Gaze out of train window with pleasurable feelings akin to ecstasy of childhood hols. But then – ah! One could lean out of the train and pick kingcups, chuffing along at 12 m.p.h., and at 4 p.m. tea was served with toasted teacakes on silver salvers. Now, one gazes out on aseptic suburbs alternating with fields so ruthlessly monochromatic, every careless cowslip and feckless fritillary must have been zapped by an Orwellian chemical spray. Only industrial wastelands are neglected and overgrown, these days. I know a dump where the wild thyme blows.

Not that one can smell the scent of thyme, or anything else for that matter, on British Rail. Fresh air is no longer permitted. Not like the good old days when every carriage window had its stout leather belt . . . But no more 1950s fetishism! For I have arrived at Manchester, whose gaze is firmly on the Olympian future.

Hotel (chosen by Charlotte) is swish and characterless. Talk achieved without undue strain, and simple supper ingested, though spectacle of all adjacent Mancunians ogling Charlotte becomes rather tedious by 9 p.m.

Make excuse and retire for early night. Too tired to watch even Sky TV news, especially as it seems to be all about transsexuals. Bad enough having to experience one sexual identity without being driven to endure the other. Whatever would I do with a penis of all things? I expect I should be constantly leaving it on the bus, as I do with my umbrella. Or find myself unable to fold it elegantly away when entering people's houses.

Flying from these vulgarities, I seek my bed, but Morpheus, though persistently paged, is elusive. Temperature of bedroom positively Saharan. Saliva, mucus, etc evaporate leaving tongue like old gardening glove. Heat zooms up defenceless nostrils, pulverising brain.

Open window, but am assailed by the sound of ongoing all-night freight wagons braking at adjoining traffic lights. Like the whinnying of great dragons. Close window, but noise seems even louder. At 6 a.m., decide it is not worth staying in bed any longer. Fall asleep, but after half-hour am awoken by machine sandblasting building opposite.

Groan aloud, though reluctant to add to cacophony. Suddenly fire alarm bursts into series of banshee shrieks. Ring Reception, and am informed that it is a false alarm and was set off by the sandblaster. There is no need to panic and they hope I was not disturbed. Decide to assert myself for once and utter a savage grumble but it is obliterated by the fire alarm's continuing aria.

Shortly after alarm finally stops, phone rings. It is Spouse, hoping I have enjoyed my refreshing break. The children are well, but he informs me his colon is misbehaving in epic style. I form the impression that it has unfurled itself majestically during the night and is towering over Rusbridge like a giant cobra, ready to strike.

'I'm seeing a specialist next week,' he announces importantly. 'Got to ring off now – my arse is buzzing again.'

Feel sudden qualm, after he has rung off, in case he really is ill. But surely not. Recall previous Spousian crises he was convinced would require heart, lung, kidney and head transplants, not to mention the conviction, in 1985, that he was being poisoned by the chair-covers.

Wait ten minutes, then ring him back. Harriet answers the phone and shouts, 'Oh goodee! It's Mummee! . . . Have you bought me anything?'

'Certainly not! Is Daddy all right?'

'Yes he's watching cricket. Mummy, can I have my ears pierced please please oh please?'

Do not wish to initiate a discussion now about the vulgarity of little girls with pierced ears, especially as I am ashamed of this little knot of resistant snobbery on my part. Pierced ears only OK on little girls if Italian. Only wish we all were.

Make an excuse, hang up and go down to breakfast. Return to find lav has been trussed up like beauty queen in paper sash saying DISINFECTED FOR YOUR PROTECTION. Should feel grateful but somehow can't.

eighteen

SPOUSE'S APPOINTMENT WITH GUT specialist. Wave him off at station with what I suspect is irritating optimism, but driving home alone afterwards am assailed with gloomy thoughts. Rehearse whole funeral complete with John Donne's *A Hymne to God the Father*, armfuls of lilies, and elegant oration by Bishop. Only problem – what to wear.

Park car and switch engine off with strange dying fall. Enter house, trying to ignore mausoleum-like stillness. Retreat into study in an attempt to escape into fiction, but am fatally arrested by old photo on wall of self and Spouse in Siena in mid-1970s, all young and intertwined.

We stayed, I recall, at the Palazzo Ravizza, and when not making love in our room overlooking ravishing Tuscan hills, amused each other by reading from T. W. Hanshew's *Cleek of Scotland Yard*, which we stole from the library. Perhaps I should offer the Palazzo a payment out of Spouse's estate, or his shade may haunt the bookcase with the memory of debts unpaid, as a dim stain defying Mrs Body's valiant dusting.

Ransack bookcase in search of Cleek, recalling with affection his man Dollops, and their breathless struggles with various fiendish criminals of exotic racial origin. Find instead another old favourite: *Labour Saving Hints and Ideas for the Home* (1925).

To Prevent a New Frying-Pan from Warping . . . Lost Knobs to Drawers . . . Blacklead is an Excellent Lubricator . . . For a Tight Screw . . . To Stiffen Lace . . . Rat Paste . . . To Revive a Shabby Silk Umbrella . . . To Renovate Old Golf Balls . . .

Wrench myself from this idyllic perusal of pre-war domestic arts and dive into Bonkbuster.

''Tes my sprang cleaning the dee, Mess Hoddle,' beamed Mrs Salmond, appearing at Fanny's door. 'If ye'll permit me, I'll replace yon lost knobs, and lubricate yeer hinges wi' blacklead. I'll stiffen yeer lace and stop up the gaps in yon skeerting boards wi' Rat Paste.'

'How kind!' exclaimed Fanny. 'Perhaps I shall go for a walk, to be out of your way.'

'Aye, lassie, do! But be sure an' take yon auld umbrella by th'door – I've just revived it wi' sugar an' boiling watter, 'twas gae shabbie!'

'How ingenious,' murmured Fanny, and winding her grey comforter about her swan-like neck, she performed a modest exit.

Black clouds were massing over Ben Heatrae as Fanny stumbled along the upland path, clutching the recently revived umbrella – of which she would soon have need, she felt sure. Some deep foreboding –

But a sudden flash of lightning rent the dark skies, and a figure rounded the rocks before her and stood silhouetted against the livid heavens. He was tall and dark, with a hint of heaviness about the face, and torment in the eyes, which suggested either habitual ill-temper or deep and secret grief.

'Young woman!' he cried in ringing . . .

Phone shrills: it is Spouse.

'I have a spastic colon,' he informs me proudly. 'He blew a lot of air up my arse and looked up it with a sort of periscope and apparently there's nothing to worry about.'

Congratulate Spouse on his spastic colon and suggest we award it asparagus and salmon to celebrate.

Spouse's relief makes him almost friendly. Remind him of Cleek of the Yard, and he vows to take me to Siena again one day. Cleek is apparently secreted in his study. After hanging up go thither to seek it and open at random.

'It is not the funeral wreath after all, you see, Miss Lorne,' said Cleek. 'It came near to being it, but it is not, it is not.' Then he laughed the foolish, vacuous laugh of a man whose thoughts are too happy for the banality of words.

How jolly true. Go out in search of asparagus.

nineteen

'*Young woman!*' *The dark, brooding figure barred Fanny's path. 'What make ye here on the slopes o'Ben Heatrae?'*

'*I – I don't make anything, sir – Father –*' *poor Fanny palpitated haplessly, for she had glimpsed, in the glimmering gloaming, the flash of a clerical collar. Could this be the fearful MacPravity of whom she had been warned by dear civilised Mr Macrae? And how exactly did one address a Scottish vicar? Reverend? Father? Pastor? MacVicar? Captain Kirk?*

'*Don't* Father *me, young woman!*' *growled the hysteric cleric, his eyebrows knotting together fearsomely like a pair of mating caterpillars. Fanny's heart gave a rebellious kick, and for a moment her ducts flooded with the adrenalin of the bare-fisted prize-fighting Hoddles of old. Her grandfather had felled Black Jack 'The Ganglion' Witherslack with a single blow, in 1852, in a field behind the Shoddy Mills at Cleckroyd.*

'*I might as well say,*' *she flared, '*don't* Young Woman *me. My name is Fanny Hoddle. And you, I take it, are . . .*'

Just a moment. *Do* caterpillars mate? I think, upon reflection, they do not. Caterpillarhood a stage of life in which mating is not attempted: rather like marriage.

Ah well. His eyebrows will have to knot together like something else mating. Must keep the mating motif however as Bonkbuster sadly lacking in that sort of thing so far. Can't seem to organise my characters towards coition. In this respect, alas, Bonkbuster all too much like everyday life.

Although Spouse, having received reprieve from suspected terminal gut-rot, is exhibiting strange new inclinations. Must beware tonight, lest, despite paunch and beard, I appear desirable.

'My colon seems quiet today,' he remarks, in the event, and breaking the time-honoured custom of centuries, rolls over to my side of the bed. There is a strange glint in his eye – a glint he normally only bestows upon the enticing spectacle of Gabriella Sabatini breaking into a sweat. 'I think it's time we revived certain quaint old rituals,' he murmurs, perusing my face with unusual absorption.

If only his colon would stir, uncoil itself, perhaps even hiss a little. But it seems sunk in serpentine slumber.

'Why, Dulcie, you have gone quite grey!' he exclaims. 'But never mind. It suits you, but why are you wearing this bloody T-shirt?'

'Cast not a clout till May be out,' I quip merrily. 'I feel the cold much more these days. But then the weather's been unusually –'

My attempt to avert amorous encounter with meteorology not effective. Spouse's nose comes in contact with my cheek. Something I used, in former days, to delight in. A nuzzle. Any word with Zs in is all right by me. But now, Oh woe –

'Listen!' I cry. 'I thought I heard a footstep! Outside, on the path! I think it's a prowler!'

'Let him prowl,' shrugs Spouse. 'It's probably only old Bernard next door giving his marrows a moonlight poke.'

'Oh God! I forgot to get some tomato plants! Can we go to the garden centre tomorrow? You can buy some chemicals to poison weeds with, as well, if you like.'

Desperate, the lengths one will go to to distract a Spouse from unwelcome attentions.

'Stop nattering, woman,' he growls. 'Can't you see I'm trying to rekindle the glowing embers of marital dalliance?'

So he thinks they're still glowing. Perhaps, despite his frequent caustic asides, Spouse is a closet optimist after all.

Close my eyes and think of Scotland.

twenty

'MUMMEE! MY TOOTH IS wobblee!'

Harriet opens her maw and waggles small fang at me.

'Do you want me to pull it out?'

'NO!'

Feel a bit like a redundant milk tooth, myself, sometimes. Hanging on by a thread.

Distracted by junk mail cascading into hall. Henry shouts, 'It looks as if the letter box is being sick!' Both children embark on extended performance of their favourite sound-effect.

'I saw a fountain once of a boy peeing!' shrieks Harriet. 'Mummy, are there any fountains of people sicking?'

'You could have a sausage machine,' suggests Henry with an evil glint, 'shaped like someone pooing!'

'For God's sake stop this disgusting talk!' I roar. 'You'd never dare to talk like this in front of Daddy, would you?'

'Well, he hits us,' Henry explains candidly.

Remember reading somewhere that corporal punishment may be made illegal, as perhaps already is the case in Holland. In this event, would Spouse's authority keel over like gigantic but hollow statue of Stalin?

Collect junk mail and retire to study (or 'sty' for short). Recall, whilst opening first envelope, picture painted by Breughel of someone being sick. But then, he was Phlegmish. Also recall Simon Schama pointing out in his book on Holland that only Dutch artists showed mothers wiping children's bottoms. The Low Countries seem to have achieved a sense of balance in things corporeal.

Perhaps hills lead to deluding ideals, whilst a flat plain landscape leads to a rational acceptance of our earthly status quo. Always associate Hitler with mountains. Spouse cannot see a hill without wanting to climb it. Whereas I cannot see one without wanting to drive round to the cool side and find a café.

The Consumers Association wants to know how I would like to spend my £$\frac{1}{4}$ million prize, should I win it. It also urges me to subscribe to *Which? Way to Health*, offering 'investigative reports about health products and services . . . a regular look at the environment and the effect it can have on your well-being'.

Shudder at the possible effect of such a publication upon Spouse, enjoying a temporary respite from hypochondria. Convinced he will soon tire of health, however – or at least, the responsibilities of the healthy. Whether his miraculously revived libido will soon flag remains to be seen. Suspect the Dutch preoccupation with sex due to lack of hills. Wordsworth, famous for his orienteering, undistinguished when it came to leering.

But to my task:

The lightning flashed, the thunder roared, and a squall of rain broke upon Fanny's pearly brow.

'My name, child, is Dougal MacPravity,' cried the dark figure, as the tempest tossed black locks across his temples. 'Come and take shelter beneath my cloak! You shall come to no harm.'

Fanny hesitated. A strong hand grasped her wrist. She looked down, and saw that a thicket of black hairs adorned the back of his hand. They were whipping about in the gale.

Why, she mused, though he wears a minister's garb, beneath he is naught but an ape!

She found the thought strangely consoling.

twenty-one

MacPravity's black cloak enveloped the palpitating Fanny. It smelt of damp Bibles, but Fanny could also feel, through the rough weave of his thrassock, the throb of his manly heart. They stumbled together down the upland path. Or up the downland path, Fanny could not tell, for the lightning flashed and the thunder roared so, that she was completely disoriented.

'Perhaps ye would find it helpful to hold on to my knobkerrie!' cried MacPravity above the storm. Fanny obeyed, clinging on for dear life.

The inconvenience of her situation galled her. She felt that conversation was required. And yet what could she say? And would it be audible?

'Do you – er – come here often?' she faltered.

'Aye, aye,' growled her companion. 'I am ever a-roaming, thro' the Braes o'Sloggie, on the screes o'Ben Heatrae. Only in the wilderness, ye ken, can ye feel the urgent pants o'the Divine.'

'Oh, how true!' exclaimed Fanny, and at that instant tripped on a tussock of Ettrick thistle and was catapulted into the minister's arms.

For an instant he held her close, and she felt his hot breath singe her eyelashes.

'I beg your pardon!' she gasped, and sought to find her feet.

'You are lucky, Mess Hoddle,' he murmured, his black eyes raking her face with a look she did not understand, 'you are lucky that I am a man unvisited by Venus!'

And he let her go. Fanny felt familiar flints beneath her boots again, but much sharper, stranger flints had sprung up in her heart.

Do flints spring up? Or are they not in fact laid down by millions of years of geological convulsion? Oh hell. The strains of fiction. Time for a hot Ribena.

Children are seated at kitchen table, upon which they have created millions of years of geological convulsion. Mrs Body is cleaning the silver and her daughter Tracey is enjoying a moment of adenoidal repose.

'Mummee!' cries Harriet, 'we've made *Neighbours*!' She proudly demonstrates that mess on table is scale model of Australian suburb, masterminded by Tracey. Express admiration.

'Our Tracey's thinkin' of goin' to Art School,' Mrs Body informs me, 'and we was wonderin' if you'd like be willin' to write her a reference.'

'Oh, certainly!' I warble, thinking of the artistic hollows Tracey has, in the past, created on our sofa. 'After all – I am a writer.' (*Of fiction*, adds private voice in my head.)

'There's tea in the pot, look,' Mrs Body cries, on seeing me put the kettle on.

'Oh, lovely!' I cry, suppressing shudder at the thought of the tarmac awaiting me in the pot. 'I'll just top it up.' (*With loose chippings*, suggests malicious voice, *and mend the path with it.*)

Harriet flings her arms around me and indulges in impetuous hug, then goes pale.

'Oh, Christ!' she exclaims. 'My bloody tooth's come out!'

She spits into my hand small tooth, and quantities of saliva and blood.

'I wonder where she's picked up that Language, then?' muses Mrs Body. Make disparaging, and entirely undeserved, remark about Rusbridge Primary.

'Congratulations, darling! The tooth fairy will be pleased!' Harriet looks distraught.

'Oh, please, Mummy! Will you write to the tooth fairy and say I want to keep my tooth? I'll miss it if she takes it away!'

Tears well, and I promise yes, of course, I will dash off a note to the supernatural one.

Spouse enters looking grim and accuses me of stealing his scissors. Conceal guilt and prepare outrageous tissue of lies in self-defence.

'You just sit down, dear,' clucks Mrs Body. 'There's nothing better after a hard morning's work than a nice relaxin' cup of tea with the family, now is there?'

Spouse twitches with Flight Response, but it is too late.

twenty-two

'MUMMEE! A BIRD HAS crapped on the car! On the windscream!'

'I prefer *pooed* if you don't mind, darling. And it's *windscreen*, actually.'

Immediately regret this intrusion of linguistic orthodoxy, at least *vis-à-vis* windscream. Harriet's malapropisms are getting few and far between, these days.

'Can I clean the car?'

'Not whilst it's parked in the street. Too dangerous.'

'Oh *Christ*! I'm never allowed to do *anything*!'

'Don't say *Christ*, Harriet. People don't like it.'

'Daddy says it.'

'Well, people don't like Daddy saying it either. I don't want you using bad language in front of anyone – *especially Mrs Body!*'

'If Jesus is the best person that ever lived, why is *Christ* bad language?'

'Mum!' Henry arrives, looking guilty in advance to save time later. 'Can I go to Julian's and sleep on the lawn in a tent next Saturday?'

'No. Er – all right.'

'Snot *fair*!' howls Harriet. 'I want to as well!'

'Don't make a fuss. I'll give you a treat of your own.'

'A Cupcake dolly?'

Harriet's eyes brighten with greed. Her current obscene object of desire is a doll who, when turned upside down, changes into a cupcake. Suspect men would also welcome women of this type.

'No, darling! Not a toy. An experience.'

'I hate experiences!' wails Harriet. 'You won't let me do anything! And you won't let me have anything! This is the worst day of my life!'

'Can I have 50p, Mum?' Henry hovers acquisitively at my elbow.

'Certainly not! What for?'

And all this time – mark the heroism – I have been attempting to unblock the S-bend below the sink. Suddenly the bung of stinking tea-leaves erupts malodorously into the bucket.

'Ugh! Pooey!'

Children retreat to other side of kitchen, pull fireblanket out of its holster and start making a den with it.

'Can we have tea in our den on the floor, Mum?'

'No! – Oh, all right. I'm busy now. Get yourself some yogurts. Have a back-to-front tea. Pudding first.'

'Ace! Brilliant!'

Children raid fridge. As fridge door is closed, a wave of fetid air wafts across the kitchen. I am haunted by domestic decay. *Memento mouldi*.

'Poo! Christ! The fridge *farted* at us, Mum!'

'Don't –'

But it is too late. Mrs Body has arrived from the bedrooms, her arms full of sheets. She glares at the children and stalks to the washing machine. Marvel that Harriet managed to combine blasphemy and obscenity in one deft phrase, but then, she has inherited my way with words. Speaking of which, I must rescue my heroine Fanny Hoddle from the cloak of the dangerous minister MacPravity – but first, the children's tea.

'Baked beans please Mum! And sweetcorn!'

Acquiesce, but transmit ferocious glare intended to convey that no mention must be made of intestinal effect of beans.

Children snigger into yogurts – an effect even more unpleasant, probably, than the full-blooded wind duet would have
been. Eventually, burdened with a cup of Mrs Body's tea, I
escape to my sty.

Pour tea into pot plant which, despite being long dead,
manages to emit a shudder. Seize pen.

*'I'll see ye to Mistress Salmond's,' announced the minister, when
they had descended as far as the flinty road that wound along the Braes
o'Sloggie to Auchtereekie. The storm had blown itself out, and
Fanny withdrew from the minister's cloak and walked demurely at his
side.*

*'Ye should take care,' he said eventually, after a prolonged and, for
Fanny, electric silence, 'not to walk on the hills alone. Much harm
could come to a young woman on the slopes of Auld Killwhillie.'*

A thrill passed through Fanny's secret veins. Was this a promise?

twenty-three

'IN THE 60S,' LAMENTS Spouse, 'I used to be able to put it off
for ten minutes by thinking of Konrad Adenauer.'

'Ah well,' I soothe, 'you don't get many politicians of that
calibre, nowadays.'

To be honest, my mind was not on the job, either, but off on
one of its linguistic forays. This time zoological, perhaps
inspired by the David Attenborough repeats. *Coypu*, for
example. Is that Aztec? Or mere Anagram? And if so, of what?

'I suppose I could try thinking of Essex Man,' ponders
Spouse. 'That would be a turn-off . . . Why don't you write a
series of bonkbusters set in Billericay? Hardy did the Wessex
novels: you could produce the Essex novels.'

Grunt in non-committal fashion, as usual when new
projects suggested by other people.

'I'll provide you with the first sentence, if you like,' offers
Spouse generously. '*Tracey was a chick just bursting to get out of
her shell-suit.*'

'Jolly good,' I sigh. 'Carry on. Don't mind me.'

Depressed, however, by Spouse's intrusive attempts to lure me away from zoological to literary speculation. *Post coypu, omnia tristia.*

Wonder, less urgently, if there are any decent anagrams of Billericay. LIBERAL . . . ICY. Oh, if only that ICY was OIK. Hence LIBERAL OIK. What would Teresa Gorman make of that tasty paradox? The problem with Liberals is their lack of Oiktitude, and vice versa. But in order to produce Liberal Oik, Billericay would have to be Billerokai. Which leads, alas, inevitably to Karaoke.

'I can't possibly write an Essex novel,' I point out crisply. 'I don't know what Karaoke is. What is it, anyway?'

But Spouse is asleep – or pretending, to avoid further discussion of Karaoke.

Wish I could sleep, but am kept awake by unearthly midnight sun. Examine places on Spouse's temples where his hair is thinning. So what if his lovemaking is premature? It matches his baldness. Although both he and I are now too old to suffer premature middle age. Wonder if this is a blessing or not, but count it just in case.

Lie awake for three and a half hours attempting to discover anagrams of kangaroo, axolotl, kookaburra and aardvark. Wish I had married David Attenborough. He is the opposite of prematurely middle-aged. Belatedly youthful. Always annoying in other people's husbands.

The view from Mr Macrae's french windows was superb. Sunlight flooded the clear Scottish peaks. Glen Gould looked close, and Glen Close looked gold. Fanny expressed admiration.

'I have always been a man of the mountains,' agreed Mr Macrae. 'In fact, every weekend I try to climb a new peak. Next Saturday I shall attempt the Huiligans. Perhaps you would care to join me?'

Fanny blushed. Her heart warmed to this mild-mannered headmaster. And yet, roaming on the Huiligans, they might meet the dreadful vicar MacPravity. Her heart shook at the thought, with something like fear.

'Or if it is raining,' Mr Macrae went on, 'perhaps you would like to join me for tea again? You might be interested in my collections of birds' eggs and pressed flowers. I have a particularly fine specimen of Vas Deferens.'

'Oh yes!' cried Fanny. 'It grows wonderfully strongly hereabouts, I have noticed.'

The door opened and Mr Macrae's sister Mairi entered and took away the tea tray.

'Would your sister not . . . care to join us?' faltered Fanny.

'Mairi suffers from agoraphobia,' explained Mr Macrae gently. 'If she stirs from the kitchen for more than five minutes, alas.'

If a man must live with his sister, mused Fanny, agoraphobia was convenient. On the other hand, no wonder he had pressed so many flowers.

'Mummy!'

Am awoken by Harriet at 6.30 a.m. declaring that she must have a poo and needs me but I must not watch, only wait without. The days of the coypoos are upon us.

twenty-four

PREVIOUS BONKBUSTER, *BIRCHES*, IS published. Tale of Charlotte Beaminster and sturdy Slavic lover. Cringe in expectation of critical opprobrium, but response is fitful and mixed. Some reviewers seem not to have noticed how bad it is. Most, thank God, seem not to have noticed it at all. One critic did, however, complain that there was not enough sex. Wholeheartedly agree.

Am interviewed by local radio station. These institutions now all dominated by huge TV monitors In Case Something Happens. Remember The End of the World was brought to you by Radio Devizes – although at present it is only cricket. Am distracted, during discussion of pulp fiction, by sight of Alec Stewart obsessively checking that he has Two Balls Left. Someone should warn him that this kind of behaviour can lead to arrest in public parks.

Invited to signing in large bookshop in centre of Warchester, where I was at school. One woman waiting – encouraging sign. She looks middle-aged. Perhaps I was at school with her daughter.

'Hello,' she beams. 'You were at school with my mother.'

Nice friendly booksellers lament lack of clientele, assure me they have advertised the event throughout Wiltshire for weeks. Assure them that the fewer customers the better as far as I am concerned, and grab shiny new copy of Pevsner.

> Area of chequered flushwork above . . . two oriels, one to the W on a much moulded bracket and with quatrefoil friezes, the other to the N semicircular . . . and on squinches.

Kind bookseller brings me a cup of tea and laments that, unless an author is of the calibre of Jilly Cooper . . . Wholeheartedly agree, and resolve to put more sex in present Caledonian bonkbuster. Or at least, more squinches.

Dive back into Pevsner, but am roused from 'Horseshoe-shaped motte . . . and circular shell-keep . . .' by small boy demanding my signature on copy of book for his father. Oblige. Boy then demands to know if I know how many breeds of toad there are in the world. Admit ignorance. Boy begins to tell me.

Beg to know his name. He informs me it is Timothy Fields and he is eight. Enquire which school he attends. Apparently Timothy does not go to school, but is taught at home, starting with half an hour's piano every morning and going on to French and, one suspects, zoology.

'Name an animal,' he implores, 'and I'll tell you about it.'

Try to ignore melancholy contrast with my own children: unmusical, frightened of spiders and not conversant with the tongues. Galled by my hesitation, Timothy begins to tell me about the Cloudy Leopard. Much struck by the poetry of this image. Ask Timothy what book he would recommend for a seven-year-old girl as Harriet is going to Gabrielle's party next week.

'That depends,' muses Timothy, 'on her interests and temperament.'

Driving home, reflect that the child is father of the man and wonder what sort of child Pevsner was. 'Name a church and I'll tell you about its complex zigzags and blind arcading'? Why are men like this? No woman I know has ever been an encyclopaedophile.

'Ah!' Mr Macrae scrambled up a heap of boulders. Dropsy! And Emphysema! And Fistula!' Eagerly he handed Fanny a small bouquet, his eyes gleaming shyly behind his glasses. Fanny raised the frail wild flowers to her face.

'*Beware, Miss Hoddle!*' *cried the headmaster.* '*Fistula is, alas, not fragrant . . . Its common name hereabouts is Stinking Hinny. It grows in the crevices . . . it is of the* Compositae, *although its umbels are not characteristic.*'

Fanny was beginning to tire of Mr Macrae's florid floriphilia. A strange feeling welled up in her spleen, and Fanny succumbed to it. Affecting to trip, she seized Mr Macrae round the neck and, falling on her back, pulled him down on top of her.

'*Och!*' *exclaimed the gentleman, and unwittingly bit her on the bosom.* '*I – do beg your pardon.*'

'*Oh, Hector!*' *murmured Fanny – but, at the next moment, a shadow fell across their recumbent forms . . .*

twenty-five

AH, THE JOYS OF high summer. Lean over to breathe in scent of glorious rose, and inhale fly. Cough guts out all over Duke of Edinburgh (the rose). There was an old woman who swallowed a fly . . . Stagger back indoors with lips firmly closed in case I should meet dog, cat, horse, etc.

'Mummee! Can we go on a picnic?'

'No! . . . Oh, all right. Just give me half an hour with my novel, first.'

'*Good day to ye, Hector Macrae.*'

MacPravity's dark bulk blotted out the sun. Mr Macrae hastened to climb off Fanny's recumbent form, offered her his hand, dusted his trousers down and polished his glasses.

'*I slipped on the scree,*' *he explained, blushing.* '*I don't think you know Miss Hoddle, our new Assistant Mistress.*'

'*Miss Hoddle and I have met.*'

MacPravity's black glittering eyes swept up Fanny's dishevelled form, loitering briefly on the heaving chaos of her magnificent chest. Then he lifted his gaze to her face, and somehow it seemed to Fanny that lightning flashed from him to her, singeing her already overtaxed bust-bodice and setting her drawers a-smoulder.

'*Perhaps it is religion,*' *she thought as hectic feelings surged through her lissom loins.* '*Perhaps Gertrude was wrong, and there is a God after all – and what I am feeling is a spiritual awakening.*'

'We were about to have a picnic,' said Mr Macrae pleasantly, having recovered his composure. 'Would you care to join us? Prawn cocktail, and so forth. Fresh from the Loch.'

Wait. Do prawns come from lochs? Hesitate over tiresome details of Natural History. Ransack bookcase but nearest thing to prawn I can find is Lobster Moth, from Readers' Digest *Nature Lovers' Library Field Guide to Butterflies and Other Insects*.

Amazed at variety of moths: Muslin Footman Moth, Ruby Tiger Moth, Poplar Kitten Moth, Puss Moth, Pebble Hook-Tip Moth . . . Realise I have always been an inadequate Mother.

'Do try one of my sister Mairi's bannocks.' Mr Macrae's head was bent over the picnic basket. But MacPravity and Fanny were oblivious to his hillside hospitality. Something magnetic and cataclysmic hovered in the air between them, that made Fanny's toes tingle in their strict little boots.

'Mummee! Picnic *now*!'

Assemble packed lunch. Stride to Spouse's study and inform him he must endure compulsory picnic. Spouse pulls horrible face and groans. Assert, not entirely convincingly, that picnics are one of the joys of high summer. Spouse retorts that the only joy of summer is the Parliamentary recess.

First few corners of Eden rejected on account of Coca-Cola cans, proximity of main road reeking with carbon monoxide, nettles, cowpats, and other of Nature's miracles. Eventually find corner of spinney on which to inflict picnic. Henry and Harriet run off into bushes to be Indians.

'Ugh! Mummee! There's some poo in here!'

'Complete with loo paper,' marvels Henry.

Déjeuner sur la Merde.

Relocate picnic in midst of huge and, one hopes, empty field. Spread blanket to protect my darlings' bottoms from ants, the caterpillar of the Hook-Tip Moth, etc. Sit down rather heavily: trouser-zip bursts with sickening report. Ground seems lower down than it used to be. Open picnic basket and beetle runs out. Harriet screams. Spouse kills it. Harriet screams even more loudly, bursts into tragic sobs and declares she wanted to keep it as a pet.

'It couldn't *help* being a beetle, Daddy!'

'If only I'd brought the Readers' Digest *Nature Lovers' Library Field Guide*,' I mused, 'we could've found out exactly what sort of beetle it was.'

'Never mind,' says Spouse as the first dollop of egg mayonnaise leaps from his sandwich and comes to rest on his corduroyed groin, 'there's always next year.'

twenty-six

FLICKING IDLY THROUGH THE TV channels, we discover *Come Dancing*. Have not seen it for twenty years, and in the interim it has evolved into a semi-pornographic parade of writhing loins. The women's dresses are now merely vestigial fins, fluttering irrelevantly in the slipstream of their nakedness. The men have cast aside the demure dicky bow and wear loose pyjamas.

'Whatever would poor dear old Victor Sylvester say?' I muse.

'Ah yes,' agrees Spouse. 'The ceremony of innocence is drowned.'

Cannot help noticing, however, that he goggles insatiably for the next twenty minutes, until Wayne and Karen Whatsit are pronounced champions. 'She's got such an effervescent personality,' bubbles the commentator, 'and they gel so well together.'

'Perhaps they gel so well together because he's got half a pint of the stuff on his hair,' remarks Spouse.

More evidence of loss of innocence next day when I discover a heap of lewd drawings in Harriet's room suggesting she is suffering from a form of penile dementia. Although left to myself I would regard it as natural, healthy curiosity, hastily throw in bin so Mrs Body will not see.

Recall tale of the British Museum long ago when Victorian prudery required the removal of all the male statues' genitalia. Order being no less important than propriety, the offending articles were meticulously catalogued and locked away in the basement. Decades later, when a more permissive climate allowed the restoration of the organs, there was consternation at the discovery that the meticulous catalogue had been lost so nobody knew which was whose. This resulted, no doubt after closing time, in prolonged and puzzled fitting sessions. A kind of antique Spot the Ball Contest.

Invited next door to meet Audrey Twill's crumbling father – a relic of the British in India, and despite his fierce appearance, an absolute Brigadear. He embarks on a series of memories along the lines of My Little Poona. Clouds of thunderflies gather above his head – evidently attracted by the sweet smell of rotting empires.

After the seventh anecdote about mouse-racing with Buffy Hurstmonceaux of the Sixth Lancers, switch on my charmed smile and mentally slink off to my wretched Bonkbuster, which alas has so far managed little in the way of erotic titillation. Indeed, the average reader would be more likely to Come Dancing.

'*Harrk!*' *Mr Macrae looked up to the clear blue Highland heaven, and his glasses flashed. '*Is that not the larrk? Do ye have larrks in Berpsover, Miss Hoddle?*'

'*Larks – oh yes. On the moors.*' *Fanny toyed with Mairi Macrae's split bannocks. She was horribly afraid hers contained a slice of haggis. She smiled at dear Mr Macrae, but was aware of the minister's silent stare burning into her bodice.* '*I think the lark –*' *she cast a swift, bashful glance at MacPravity,* '*– is as near as one can get to spirituality incarnate. Don't you?*'

'*What a charming thought!*' *cried Mr Macrae, clasping his hands and beaming at her. But the minister scowled.*

'*Ye canna say sic a thang aboot yon capercaillie,*' *he growled, indicating, with a curt nod, a strange bird crouching in the heather some fifty yards away. As Fanny watched, the bird stood up on tiptoe, inflated two rosy pouches on either side of its beak, shook its tail and emitted a loud noise like the breaking of wind, which ricocheted among the rocks in which the picnickers sheltered.*

'*That,*' *commented MacPravity sourly,* '*is to attract the females.*'

'*You sound disapproving,*' *faltered Fanny with a strained laugh.*

'*I incline to St Cuthbert's view of womankind,*' *commented MacPravity, and sank his teeth into a slab of blood pudding.*

What? Still no bonking? Must get rid of tiresome Macrae.

Then, with a violent rumble, a thunderous mass of leaping rock swept down the bare slopes of Glen Close, and, to Fanny's horror, swept Mr Macrae into the abyss.

twenty-seven

HARRIET'S END-OF-TERM school play: a sci-fi fantasy in which schoolchildren are blasted into outer space. Pretty widespread fantasy among both teachers and parents, I should think. Needless to say, Harriet is one of the aliens. On the morning of the performance, she warns me that when she gets home afterwards she will have to wash her face to get rid of the make-up cleansing cream.

'Wash your face?' I enquire. 'We've never tried that before – I wonder how it's done?'

'Oh *shut up*, Mummy, you're *embarrassing me!*' she hisses. Often think she would prefer a proper Mummy with high heels and cooking. *Cuisine minceur*.

On the way to school, coasting down a certain hill, a car coming in the opposite direction flashes its headlamps at me. Am instantly seized with motor neurosis. What is wrong? One of my tyres on fire? Radiator about to explode? Peer anxiously at dashboard. Or was it old friend in the other car? Peer anxiously in mirror. Then round corner and – shock horror! Speed trap.

Cop gives me suspicious glare. Tempted to leap out of car, fall to my knees and confess to speeding, planting bombs, anything. Luckily motor neurosis has slowed me to pre-occupied crawl. All the same, it takes ten minutes to get rid of the surplus adrenalin. On the way back, wonder if I in turn should flash people coming in the opposite direction. Seems a neighbourly act. But on the other hand, why should nasty dangerous speed freaks get away with it?

Resolve not to flash dirty transit vans driven by scowling young men with earrings, only middle-aged women like myself. Then recall that worst driver I know is a middle-aged woman: Alice. In the end do not flash anybody: would make a hash of it and flash police car, probably.

At home, remind Spouse that tonight it is Harriet's play. He frowns.

'I don't think I'd better come,' he warns. 'I was woken up at dawn by someone shouting "Eric! . . . Eric!" and it turned out to be my own colon.'

In other words, the return of irritable bowel syndrome – or in Spouse's case, coloratura colon – just in time to save him from ordeal of school play.

'Harriet would hate it,' he adds artfully, 'if my colon started to rumble loudly in a quiet poignant bit.' Reply that there never are quiet poignant bits in school plays. Spouse retorts that due to tendency of children to forget lines, there is usually nothing else.

'There you are!' he adds triumphantly. 'It shouted ERIC again just then!'

Pointless to deny hearing anything. Spouse quite capable of producing other, more melodramatic symptoms, if Eric not enough to excuse him from school play.

Sigh and withdraw to study where have just got rid of irritating protagonist by means of a Scottish landslide. Unfortunately, landslides rare in Rusbridge.

'Oh, Dougal!' cried Fanny, clinging desperately to Pastor MacPravity and sobbing into the folds of his clerical clothing. 'How horrible! Poor, dear Mr Macrae!'

'The picnic-basket, too,' observed MacPravity, 'how symbolic of the vanity of human wishes.'

'Is there nothing we can do?' cried Fanny wildly, flinging a despairing glance over the precipice over which Mr Macrae had so suddenly and violently disappeared.

'Diarmid Fannich will see to it,' MacPravity sighed. 'The mountain guide.'

Wait. Did MacPravity speak in Scots dialect? Liberally dot his recent utterances with ochs, th's and ye kens. Time he stopped all this prattling anyway and got down to the serious business of fin-de-siècle Caledonian bonking – if such a thing ever existed.

Harriet's play excellent. Inform Spouse he missed a treat. He replies with mock-tragic smug shrug. Increasingly irritated by Spouse's ability to get away with murder, and own inclination to confess to ones I have not committed. So far, anyway. But he'd better not push his luck.

twenty-eight

SCHOOL HOLIDAYS SET IN with a vengeance. Children acquire a video of *Robin Hood: Prince of Thieves* and sit down to watch it. Anxiety about the almost continuous sounds of designer violence mitigated by gratitude at its power to absorb. Whilst children agog, get on with urgent tasks, i.e. lying on bed and reading Burlington Catalogue.

Become convinced that what is missing from my life may turn out to be polyester. Struck by the idea of 'Official Replica Shirts'. Tempted to get Spouse Great Britain Rugby League shirt (material: polyester) adorned with flashy British Coal logo.

Surprised that there should still be such a thing as British Coal. Had assumed the rich seams had petered out, as with Lymeswold. Wonder if the thing that is missing from my life may turn out to be Arthur Scargill. Feel guilty that I am lounging about, but recollect that Spouse is lazing in garden listening to cricket. Cricket infinitely preferable on the wireless especially now cricketers and pitch are emblazoned with advertising slogans.

Sportsmen have become billboards, and now, by sporting Official Replica Shirts, couch potatoes can become sportsmen. Flick through a few more pages of catalogue and am amazed by the writing on the trainers. Perhaps it is a vain attempt to do something about adult literacy. Thousand of years hence, will a solitary trainer be the only relic of our civilisation, and provide the key to our philology, like the Rosetta Stone?

Feel guilty that I have surrendered to this encroachment of language so far as to acquire a sweatshirt adorned with the cryptic exhortation PUMA FUNCTION. Presumably I am intended to live up to my sweatshirt by imitating the action of a tiger. Comfort myself with the thought that, were pumas people, for every ten minutes they spent haring down the high street tearing people's heads off, they would devote three or four days to lying on the bed reading the Burlington Catalogue.

'Mummee! I want to be an outlaw when I grow up!'

'Mum! Can we make a tree house in the garden?'

'Yes – er, no! You might hurt yourselves! Come back!'

Recall complacently that Spouse is in the garden, and if they hurt themselves, he will hardly be able to avoid some soupçon of responsibility. Also aware that only tree in the garden is ancient plum, too frail to accommodate dwelling for anything more substantial than a tit.

Sigh at the recollection that, due to school hols, Bonkbuster has stalled at promising moment and my heroine Fanny's bodice must remain tantalisingly unripped. Stare at ceiling and discern stain thereon shaped like India. Wonder if I shall ever go to India and think perhaps not. This year it is to be Thetford (Centerparcs – palm trees and water slides enclosed in helpful glass dome). Passage to Thetford is to be my destiny. Ay me.

Loud sounds below indicate arrival of children in garden and indignation of Spouse thereat. Stick head out of window, express sympathy, and offer cup of tea. Spouse requests his Panama hat. From up here I notice his bald patch is spreading, like hole in ozone layer. Remember seeing Panama hat in attic and set off with sense of adventure.

Attic is dark, hot, seething with alien life: rather like India. Or indeed Sherwood Forest. Stare fascinated at eaves and timbers and realise we do live in a tree house after all. Doubt if children will find this thesis convincing, however.

Find Panama hat, but it has been eaten by mice, or possibly – horrors – rats. Aunt Elspeth, donor of hat, expected at some point during school hols so damage to hat a disaster and its replacement by Official Replica an urgent necessity. Immediately convey it to Spouse and express consternation as it is a male duty to protect us from rats as well as build tree houses, both of which he has wilfully neglected.

Spouse is making a bow and arrow for Henry and serenely ignores the Panama problem. Harriet is busy with mud pies.

'I'm Maid Marian, Mummy. I'm doing the cooking!'

Heart sinks. Declare I am sure I saw Maid Marian fighting at some stage in aforementioned epic.

'Oh yeah!' cries Harriet and hurls herself into fight with

54

Henry which as usual ends in tears. Spouse gives me old-fashioned look.

'Where's that tea you promised us, then?'

twenty-nine

HENRY INVITED TO GO and sleep on Julian's lawn within tent. Sounds reassuringly suburban, though the Rainge-Roughvers' lawn more of a savannah: wild and rolling and patrolled by Great Danes which blot out the sun.

'He'll be all right,' soothes Spouse from behind the *Observer* (how acute was my temptation, at the newsagent's, to buy some tabloid rubbish instead). 'After all, he is nearly a teenager.'

Dare not confess that this is precisely what's bothering me. Already Henry is spending more time in his room, alone with what one must charitably conclude must be his thoughts.

'But, you know . . . er . . . smoking, and girlie mags, and so on.'

'What are girlie mags?' cries Harriet, leaping up from her toy hospital and closing down a whole ward with a single kick. 'Can I have one?'

'Girlie mags never did anyone any harm.'

Spouse yawns, as if to demonstrate his serene indifference to girlie mags.

'They're part of the monstrous apparatus of patriarchy,' I object, aware that, as usual at such moments, I am quoting Alice.

'What's the monstrous apparatus of patriarchy, Mummy? Is it to do with horror? Can I have one?'

'Don't come the Clare Short with me,' sighs Spouse.

'Clare Short is wonderful!' I cry indignantly, having heard her on *Desert Island Discs* and therefore absolutely sure of my facts.

'Who's Clare Short, Mummy? Has she got long hair?'

'No!'

'And you can't have one,' adds Spouse.

Though if little girls played with Shorties rather than Sindies, they would get a much sounder start in life.

Harriet screams and runs out into the garden, to vent the fury of her thwarted covetousness upon even lower forms of life. She leaves the debris of the toy hospital all over the floor. Tidy it away, feeling that my actions are pregnant with symbolic meaning, these days, usually to do with the dismantling of the debris of civilised society. But I suppose the school holidays are a bit like that.

'You shouldn't clear up after her all the time,' objects Spouse.

'Why not?' I retort wearily. 'I clear up after you all the time.' Semi-satisfying moment.

Later, Harriet corners me in the garden where I am hacking ineffectually at the bindweed.

'Mummy,' she announces, 'I'm not really a child any more, am I?'

Express surprise. She is, after all, only seven.

'No I'm not a child any more, Mummy! I'm turning into a kid! I like jeans now don't I? And trainers. And Kate Bush and other kids' type of music. Not stupid old Humpty Dumpty.'

Somewhere high up, windswept and symbolic, poor Humpty Dumpty quivers and topples. Feel enormous sadness, sit down, and draw Harriet to what, were there any justice in the world, would be my ample bosom.

'Darling,' I whisper, choking back the tears, 'don't be in such a hurry to grow up. Being a child is a wonderful, precious—'

'But I'm not allowed to *do* anything!' she roars, and with one mighty heave, hurls me on to my back and runs off impatiently to be a new improved Kid.

Inverted and helpless like a turned turtle, I survey the summer sky. Suddenly the face of Mr Twill Next Door appears between my legs – for what I hope will be the only time. He is flourishing the first marrow with foolish pride and hands it over to me. Heroically conceal dismay and project delight and gratitude. Sometimes I think if I'd married Prince Charles there wouldn't have been all this trouble.

Backing gratefully and gracefully up the garden path, I trip on one of Harriet's discarded toys, totter sideways and bash my head on the door of the garden shed. Wish I were politician so I could present this as a great triumph.

Balefully glare at marrow in privacy of kitchen, and wish it was a courgette. Who was it who said Ripeness is all? Bloody fool.

thirty

AUNT ELSPETH COMETH, COMPLETE with three vast photograph albums of her grandchildren.

'Gabrielle with chicken pox, poor little mite.' Child resembles Victorian pudding of the sultana variety. 'And that's one of her on the beach at Muchnapukie.' Child resembles Victorian pudding of the plain variety. 'There's Hazel – now hasn't she got a lovely little figure?' Glare at photo of slim and pretty woman wearing shiny satin bikini and agree, between clenched teeth.

'She got her figure back straight away after Gabrielle, it was those post-natal exercises, dear.' Aunt gives me a sharp, mock-innocent look, averting her eyes from the rolling acres of my Midlands. OK, so I'm over ten stone again, but I am quite tall, dammit. With my heels on, anyway. We can't all be elves and demi-puppets, Aunt.

The litany of praise for her daughter-in-law continues in the kitchen, however.

'Hazel does the cleverest things with left-overs, dear.' Aunt observes my attempt to smuggle from fridge to waste-bin some slices of ham which have acquired a blue shimmer which would be more becoming on the Aegean. 'Mind you, she did do that Cordon Bleu course.' Find, and stifle horror at, putrefying cucumber. 'She made a wonderful *crème brûlée* once.'

Admit that my acquaintance with *crèmes* is marginal only, though I am increasingly tempted by the thought of *crime passionel*. Or is it *passionelle*? Tiresome French. Obsessed with the sex of their endings. Thank God one belongs to a sexless nation. Have noticed a creeping tendency to agree with Lady Thatcher on recent occasions and suspect I may be in the process of desiccation.

'Cream *passionel* – is that with passion fruit, dear? Hazel made us a wonderful passion fruit gateau last weekend.'

Tempted to insert putrefying cucumber into the aforementioned Hazel, but luckily she is hundreds of miles north. Hope it is raining there.

'Alistair must be getting fat.'

'Och no, no, dear. He's like his father.' Aunt lapses into complacent contemplation of the thinness of her late husband.

'Mummmee!' Harriet runs in. 'I want to be a vampire when I grow up!' Aunt purses lips. Suspect the divine Hazel has already put her children's names down for employment at the bank. Harriet turns to Aunt and bares her fangs. 'Can I suck your blood, Auntie?'

'I think,' observes Aunt rising, 'it is time for my sleep.'

She goes. Give Harriet sudden violent hug. She sinks her teeth into my neck. A struggle ensues, which I lose.

'Stop it! Stop it! Or you'll bloody kill me and we won't be able to go to Centerparcs!'

'You said *bloody*, Mummy!'

'If you're a vampire you shouldn't care!'

Yes, Centerparcs. A tropical paradise under a glass dome in Thetford Forest. We hope. Spouse encouraged by the supposed proximity of Norfolk churches, Neolithic flint mines, knapped flint, samphire, etc. Am myself eagerly anticipating on-site cafés and queueing for the Jacuzzi.

Spouse enters tenderly blowing dust off old book. Never performs the same kindly office for old wife.

'Listen to this,' he says. 'It's Pevsner. *The great days of Thetford are over.*'

Seize Pevsner and peruse. Am attracted by the thought of the church of St-Mary-the-Less. Feel pang of fellow-feeling for her. Suspect she may have had a cousin-in-law called Hazel.

After enjoying auntless cup of tea, retire to study to make list of things I must pack. But first:

'Mr Macrae's puir sister, Mairi!' lamented Mrs Salmond, as Fanny laced up her boots. 'She'll be comforted to see ye, nae doot. Och! The way that woman worked. She was up at five scrubbin' the step —'

But soon Fanny was on the road. The Macrae house crouched beneath the tawny slopes of Glen Close, a spiral of smoke rising from its chimney. No doubt even now, in the height of her grief, Mairi Macrae was performing a whole range of dextrous domestic duties.

But – oh horror! A massive report echoed around the Glen, and the whole house, it seemed to Fanny, shivered for a moment before rising into the air and blowing itself to bits.

thirty-one

SPOUSE AWOKEN EARLY BY his bowel. Enquire, with a sigh, what it said this time.

'It said, "Bonk bonk bonk in Warrington."'

'Perhaps it's part of an English Tourist Board Campaign – to encourage people to visit the north.'

We have come east, to a Holiday Village in Thetford Forest. The intention is that Harriet shall learn to swim and that Spouse will impart to Henry the secret of manly sports.

'What are we doing here?' moans Spouse, glaring at the ceiling. 'I thought we hated people.'

Annoyed that Spouse should absorb me into his misanthropy. Would prefer tasteful misanthropy of my own. Also secretly quite like villa, which Spouse says resembles food processor. Deep joy of single beds.

'Mum it's brilliant!' cries Henry from the TV remote control. 'You press the question-mark key and if there's any messages for you they come up on the screen.'

Rather dashed to hear that the outside world can pursue us even in the depths of our food processor.

We are further liquidised later in the day in the subtropical swimming paradise. Beam at Great British Public enjoying themselves: freckly grans, whippety nymphs, the youth all wearing asymmetrical fluorescent shorts. Attempt to hate them, but fail. Find whole spectacle rather touching.

'Don't you think Bath must have been rather like this? In the eighteenth century? All these people having fun?'

At the word *fun*, Spouse's face sets like concrete.

'Why are all these kids so well behaved?' he growls. Suspect they are all lower middle class and therefore tidied into timidity.

Take to the water: Henry assuming sole responsibility for middle-middle-class hooliganism. Harriet discards armbands and develops a worrying tendency to swim downwards.

'Bubby! I'b swimmig udderwater!'

Hover nearby, trying to hide flab and foreboding. Sure enough, at 3 a.m. the following morning:

'Ear! Oh ear! Ear hurts! Ow ow ow!'

'What? Was that my bowel?'

No my Lord. Only your daughter.

Later, queue at Medical Centre with others damaged by diversion, including unfortunate girl who has fallen on her snorkel. Harriet writhes on my lap howling, *How Much Longa?* Other angelic little lower-middle-class girls sit bravely biting their lips, twiddling their earrings and refraining from public pain.

Eventually Doctor gazes into Harriet's orifices (by gum they earn their money, these medics), diagnoses tonsillitis and prescribes banana-flavoured antibiotic mixture, which Harriet remembers from last time, with a retch and a curse.

Spouse and Henry are playing tennis with a man called Jeremy and his sons Sebastian and Lysander. Evidently not lower middle class. Harriet ('Ow ow my ear! It's all the Lord's fault!') and I wait outside the netting. Spouse serves double fault and hisses, *Take her away!*

Return to villa and offer Harriet Roald Dahl's *Big Friendly Giant* – attractive alternative to the Lord. She prefers TV, however.

'Mummee! There's a message for us!'

The Lord seems to have had a particularly active morning: Aunt Elspeth has had a stroke and Spouse is requested to attend her deathbed. Drive him to Peterborough where he catches the train north. Return to Thetford where Henry and Harriet are being entertained by the mother of Sebastian and Lysander – an Ann, which perhaps explains it. Delightful woman. Thoughts of Peterborough lead her to confide that she went to Oundle once, and there was an exhibition of small organs in the marketplace.

Henry enquires if Aunt Elspeth is dead yet. Reply that we must wait for Daddy to get in touch. Harriet bursts into feverish tears and declares she wishes she was dead too.

Tonsillitis worse. Drive home takes seven hours through torrential rain. Message on answerphone: Aunt Elspeth pronounced clinically dead, then sat up moments later and asked for egg and chips. Will take me a lot longer to recover from holiday than it took aged Aunt to recover from death.

thirty-two

SPOUSE RETURNS FROM SCOTLAND now that Aunt Elspeth has escaped the jaws of the Grim Reaper with barely a rip in her herringbone skirt.

'It wasn't really a proper stroke,' he muses. 'More a sort of nasty turn. Her heart did actually stop, though. And she claims she had one of those out-of-body experiences.'

Lucky old Elspeth. An out-of-kitchen experience would do for me.

'Makes you think,' ponders Spouse, staring into his Lapsang, 'about Death.'

Beg him to cheer up, as he is unlikely to die today.

'Ah, but nobody can actually guarantee that, can they?' He gives me sombre look. 'I think I'm going to start taking sugar again.'

'Touch-a touch-a touch-a *touch* me / I wanna be *durdee*!' trills Harriet from the table, where she is busy drawing modern ballet performed by women with extremely long hair. Spouse raises eyebrow.

'She found my old *Rocky Horror* tape. But I've bribed her not to sing it when Mrs Body's around.'

'Mum,' Henry approaches me looking disturbed. 'What's an out-of-body experience? Is it like astral travel?'

Inform him that if I ever find out, I shall let him know – by a series of mysterious knockings, if necessary.

Withdraw to study, as it is even more Spouse's turn than usual. After all, whilst I was struggling with kids, holiday, tonsillitis, etc, he was enjoying leisurely Caledonian deathbed – nay, opposite of deathbed, as it turned out. Liferaft, perhaps.

Besides, my heroine Fanny urgently needs rescuing from her own excessive accumulation of Caledonian mortalities. Feel I may have been a little gratuitous in making Mairi Macrae's house explode, and strike out last two paragraphs.

Fanny will have to perform sympathetic visit therefore to grieving sister of the deceased.

'And they still haven't . . .' Fanny hesitated tactfully.

'Found the body? No.' Mairi's face was deathly white, and her hand shook as she passed Fanny a plate of her finest warm bannocks.

'How distressing for you!' exclaimed the tender-hearted Fanny, declining nourishment. 'I know you and your brother were unusually close.'

'I know you and he were unusually close, too,' rejoined Mairi, with a strange flash of her semi-precious sea-green eyes. 'Perhaps you would like to help yourself to a keepsake from amongst his little knick-knacks.'

'In due course, I thank you . . .' Fanny dropped her eyes to the Turkish carpet. 'These landslides! It makes one feel, does it not, particularly vulnerable.'

Mairi sighed. A small spider fell into Fanny's tea. She began to think it was time she withdrew.

Her farewells said, and her condolences repeated, she set off with relief into a stiff northerly breeze blowing straight down off the Swoons o'Crawlkerbie. After the still, close house of death she wished to be buffeted by the living wind.

'Miss Hoddle!'

A familiar figure appeared from behind an oolitic extrusion. Fanny looked up. The rugged countenance of the Pastor gazed down at her, and his glowing cheeks and flashing eyes seemed part of the very pulse of the planet. He seized her hands. Fanny's heart leapt.

'The lav's bunged up again. Fancy a cuppa?'

Annoyed by interruption, though encouraged by Spouse's cheerful tone. Suspect he has skirted round the black chasms of whatsit and emerged into daylight.

'You'll have to ring that plumber johnnie of yours.'

Huge twang of heartstrings and audible blush sweep me down emotional landslide. Drop pen under table to permit brief retreat whilst casually supposing that Tom has gone abroad.

'Well, any old plumber will do, for God's sake.'

Emerge to find that the summer afternoon has given way to strange plangent breeze, slanting Vermeer light, and autumnal smell of decay.

thirty-three

CANNOT FACE SUMMONING PLUMBER from Tom's old outfit –
Buddhist/Anarchist Plumbing Collective.

'I think we'll stick to ordinary bog-standard plumbers this
time,' I announce with hypocritical sigh.

'I should think so too. Frankly, I could never understand
what you saw in that bloke. New Age dimwit.'

Bite tongue and rifle through Yellow Pages. Choose
plumber boasting of his membership of ancient order; presumably founded by the chaps who installed Claudius's central
heating. He turns out to have yellow teeth and large paunch,
but I firmly refuse to brood tenderly on memories of the
dimwit's sweet breath and springy young midriff.

Whilst plumber is doing things with poles to manholes
outside – making him look, briefly, like stranded gondolier – I
inspect my tongue in bathroom mirror. It suggests something
out of *Alien*. Wish I hadn't bitten it, but alternative was a rash
outburst of plain speaking to which I am not convinced
Spouse would have been equal. Sigh deeply. Apart from
anything else, it is the end of the cricket season.

New school uniform waits in vain for name-tapes to be
sewn in. Mist hangs over the blackberries. The robin sings his
autumn –

'Mum! We looked down the manhole and it was really
gross! There was piles and piles of –'

'I don't want to know! You two stay indoors until the
plumber's finished. You might catch something!'

'What?' Harriet looks incredulous. 'A *fish*?'

Eventually regain the peace and quiet of my study. The
sense of bunged-up debris, both visible and invisible, has risen
to my eyebrows. This calls for radical dam-busting.

*'At last!' Dougal MacPravity's breath singed her tender earlobe:
his teeth closed, gently but conclusively, around her neck, whilst his
fingers tore at the twenty-seven jet buttons which kept her bosom
modestly encased in grey gaberdine. Fanny almost swooned, but the
rough outcrop of rock digging into her tender left kidney somehow kept
nudging her back on to the right side of consciousness.*

*Suddenly MacPravity's patience snapped, and the Braes o'Sloggie
echoed to the deafening report of Fanny's ripped bodice. The twin,*

quivering orbs of her nakedness burst upon a waiting world. For a moment the landscape seemed to hold its breath: then, an eagle plummeted out of the sky and dashed its brains out upon a nearby rock; the waterfalls boiled, the gorse gasped, and MacPravity fell to his knees with an inarticulate sob.

A small boy appeared around the pinnacle of rock known locally as Auld Stinkie. He stopped: his mouth dropped open, and he proffered an envelope to Fanny, who drew her discarded cloak around her with magnificent elan and addressed him in proud and confident tones.

'I was just giving the minister Artificial Respiration,' she said. 'He almost drowned in the waterfalls.'

'Mestress Salmond said I would find ye on the mountain,' gasped the small boy. 'The letter –'

'Yes, yes. Thank you. Now go!' cried Fanny, irritated by this juvenile intrusion. But the boy hovered, evidently expecting a tip.

'I have no money!' said Fanny. 'Be off!'

'Just – one more peep at yon chest?' stammered the child.

Fanny's temper exploded. She flung the cloak aside. The boy took one fearful glance and ran off screaming down the scree.

She ripped the letter open, and what she read threw her heart into such violent throbs, her whole frame reverberated to its panic.

'Feyther very ill accident in mill come home at once Mother.'

'Mummee! The man's finished! The loo's working but you can still smell poo in the garden!'

Lay pen aside, embrace child, and accompany her outdoors to admire the smell of sewage. Spouse is shaking his head over the last of the windfalls.

'We should have picked these,' he laments with accusing look. Then he sticks a finger in his ear. 'Needs syringing,' he sighs. 'Can't hear a thing. Silting up. Still, waste not, want not. I'll bring it home and you can put it on your compost heap.'

thirty-four

'I must go!' Fanny shook MacPravity's shoulder. He groaned, stirred, and raised up his head: his eyes, however, remained closed.

'Put them away,' he gasped, clutching convulsively at her sleeve. Fanny drew her cloak more firmly across her chest.

'I am dressed,' she hissed. 'But I must go! My father is unwell! An accident! At the mill!'

Leaving her lover floundering among the Nipplewort, Fanny ran off down the hillside, and was soon at Mrs Salmond's. The good woman's powerful Celtic telepathy had foreseen trouble, and she had packed Fanny's bag. Mrs Salmond, however, exclaimed at the damage to Fanny's clothing. Her bodice was comprehensively ripped.

'I was caught,' blushed Fanny. 'Upon the gorse, alas.'

'I've an auld funeral bodice ye can borrow,' soothed Mrs Salmond. Luckily she was a woman of mighty girth. Fanny buttoned on the bodice, her heart racing. No sooner had a lover's lips feasted on her palpitating cheeks, than her father was on his deathbed. How cruel Fate was!

'Archie's bringing the trap roond,' said Mrs Salmond. 'Th'train leaves the Creels o'Faucht in half an huir.'

The sound of hooves and wheels whirled in Fanny's ears, and soon she was resting her head against the soot-scented pillows of a third-class seat on the Great Northern Steam Locomotive, Auld Crankie. She drew a deep breath, and for a while she sought to compose her madly beating heart by repeating, over and over again, the strange exotic names of the stations they passed through.

Killiebogie. Rothietiftie. Knocknamuir. Kuirnbeefhash. Maggie-oustie. Knickertie-Knackertie.

Alas, they only reinforced her sense that this was a foreign country, and that her lover – she thought, now, she might call him that – was, and forever would be, a stranger to her. But how could she think of a lover at a time like this, when her father lay – perhaps maimed, perhaps dead? Her imagination reeled at it.

After a while, the need to relieve her feelings made her reach inside her reticule. She brought out pen and paper. She must share her thoughts with Gertrude.

Am getting a bit bored with all this sub-Balmoral stuff. Interesting that Balmoral rhymes with amoral. Nevertheless, there is something irrevocably unsexy about Scotland, despite the kilts, which are a red herring. I should have sent Fanny off to Tuscany. Then MacPravity could have been a Catholic priest with olive-black eyes to match his smouldering soutane. They could have cavorted beneath figs, vines and cypresses instead of having to grapple upon gorse and granite. Am cruel to my heroine – but then, so was Hardy. At least I haven't blinded, drowned or dishonoured anyone yet. Er – not in fiction, at least.

Anyway, it's too late to change it now. Have been led astray, *vis-à-vis* Scotland, by the Shadow Cabinet. I suppose it is too much to hope that eventually the electorate will be, too.

Writing bonkbusters a long, hard slog. Wish I were In Films. Salivate over thought of a feminist version of *The Three Musketeers* starring Princess Anne, Martina Navratilova and Virginia Wade – shot in Tuscany.

Shoes hurt so kick them off, and observe blister on big toe, caused by new suede slip-ons, bliss in shop and torture ten minutes later. Put plaster on toe, feeling sorry for it. I don't have the bottle to send it winging joyously up the backsides of bureaucrats. It is a toe whose time may never come.

House strangely quiet. Normally at moments like this child runs in crying Mummee! Henry's killed it! Or Promise not to be angry but. School holidays, however, have ended. Moment for which entire population gasps – except, presumably, teachers.

And yet . . . how apt this solitude and silence is to engender melancholy. Especially as Spouse has gone to Oxford for nostalgic bout of Bodleian and boozing. Shudder at the thought of being fossilised in academe. But then, no worse than being fossilised in a suburb not far from Swindon.

Switch off word-processor. Life must have more to offer than this. Hence loathed Melancholy. Four whole hours before I have to collect kids. Grab jacket and go off in search of adventure.

thirty-five

SOON ABANDON HOPES OF an adventure in the few hours before the school run, mainly due to lack of funds. If only I had money or guns I might have managed some modest diversion. Content myself with an ice-cream version of a chocolate bar, and manage to remove all traces of it from my person before collecting Harriet at 3.30.

'Is Daddy still away in Oxford?'

Make affirmative, disenchanted and jealous reply.

'When we get home can I play with dough please please please?'

'Yes – *no!*'

'Too late you promised! Hee hee!'

Prepare dough for children and decide to withdraw as I cannot bear to watch.

'Look Mum I've made a lady!'

'Yes darling – I'm going up to tidy the attic now.'

'Now I'm going to make a tart of her!'

Attic is calm, quiet and dusty. Wonder if it is emblem of the Unconscious. No need to rush out seeking adventure on the streets when I can blow the dust off Spouse's old love letters – both of them. Perhaps also find unsuspected Rembrandt.

Searching for Rembrandt, notice box containing Spousian seminar papers brought back from USA last summer and not yet unpacked. Unpromising source of adventure, but open lid and rifle through top geological layer. 'Education and the Non-Conformist Tradition in Late-Seventeenth-Century Leighton Buzzard' . . . 'Neo-Aristotelian Elements in the Philosophy of Mercantile Aggrandizement, 1680–1689' . . . 'Marlene's Love Palace: Tits'n'Ass Nitely'.

What?!?

No, it was not an hallucination. Here, deftly secreted between sheets of flawless academe, is a rather glossier offering from Marlene – adorned with representation of girl who has not seen her feet since puberty – or, possibly, since The Operation. Boggle and blush, even though I am alone. Try to imagine Spouse in the company of such a creature, and feel sick. Wonder if I am jealous and outraged, and if so, what this means. Am I still in like with him? Or is it purely a feminist qualm? Wonder if the girl (Cindee Jane) would enjoy a more fulfilling life as a carpenter, gas fitter or even historian.

The swine will be back from Oxford tomorrow. If indeed it is the Bodleian and not the bodily which detains him. Essential to keep my dignity and humiliate him, but have bad track-record and suspect I may only accomplish the opposite. Shove *Tits'n'Ass Nitely* up my jumper, rush downstairs and address myself to my *œuvre*.

Dearest Gertrude, Fanny wrote, the rhythm of the train assisting her quaint italic script, I trust all is still idyllic with you at Aix-à-Lauvère, and that M. Boursin continues in his elegant Gallic attentions. I often think of you drinking Baume de Venise upon his veranda, and bestowing the treasures of your mind upon his lovely daughters Françoise-Eloise and Violette-Emanuelle.

But O, Gertrude, such catastrophes have befallen me in your absence! You recall I wrote of the dear modest headmaster who befriended me, Mr Hector Macrae, who showed me his collection of birds' eggs? Well, but two days ago, as we were picnicking with the minister Mr Dougal MacPravity, a landslide swept Mr Macrae awae – I mean, away, pray excuse my spelling, I am so distraught! His body has never been found, but you can imagine my distress! I have been much comforted, however, by the minister, who despite a rather sinister appearance – but never mind that.

In the midst of his consolations, my dear Gertrude, I received an urgent summons home, for my father has been injured in a mill accident and lies at this moment, for aught I know, at death's door! I write this in the train, going south – forgive me, my tears blot the paper . . .

Essential not to get *Tits'n'Ass* out of proportion. On the other hand, I'll kill him! Prowl about the house planning, and rejecting, various ingenious revenges and speeches of coruscating irony. How could he! Out chasing Tits'n'Ass nitely, whilst, oceans away, I kept the home fires – well, never mind what I was up to. At least that was the real thing.

The day he returns from Oxford, I shall place Marlene's ghastly menu, complete with capering tart, beneath the bedcover, on his pillow.

thirty-six

Poor Fanny threw her handkerchief over her face and wept. Then, lulled by the rhythm of the train's wheels, she slept. When she awoke, the names of the stations had taken on a more familiar music: Cleckthorpe, Gulpwell, Dronspit, Grindlow, Goytre. Soon they would arrive at Berpsover. Fanny smoothed Mrs Salmond's funeral bodice over her distraught young heart, and hoped the loan of the garment would not prove to be disastrously appropriate.

'How did it happen?' Fanny murmured, stroking her father's knotted brow.

'T'ruddock exploded,' he replied in a low, broken voice, 'and t'blew t'becketts apart, see? T'kinnocks dropped off, and I were hit in't withers bi a flyin' hewitt.'

'You'd been worried about that ruddock for years, hadn't you, Feyther?'

'Ay, lass. But nivver mind about that now. Wilt tha . . . sing to me?' His gnarled old hand found hers, and closed over it.

'Oh, willingly, Feyther.' Fanny cleared her throat, and began. 'The People's Flag is —'

'Nay, nay, not that,' he interrupted her. 'Sing me . . . summat in that thar French.'

'Why, Feyther!' Fanny's eyes filled with tears. 'I had never thought to —'

'I'm reet proud o'me educated daughter,' the old man muttered, his cheeks wet in the faint flicker of the light from the tiny window, beyond which loomed the dark mass of the Guscott and Pikelet Steel Truss Company. 'Now, lass, sing on.'

Fanny hesitated, trying to think of something in French. For a moment she could only remember Frère Jacques, but she felt that might be a little too robust for a deathbed.

'Mummee! Daddy's come home!'

Has he, indeed. Smile sinisterly at the thought of the surprise awaiting him at bedtime: the lewd brochure from Marlene's Love Palace now reposing on his pillow.

'So. How was Oxford?'

'Absolutely ghastly.'

Attempt for a moment to recall any occasion during the past ten years when Spouse has willingly admitted experiencing pleasure. No doubt when confronted with memories of Marlene's he will manage to dredge up a shudder from the murky depths of his hypocrisy. It will be, 'Oh, that dump – Rick Dill dragged me off there one night when he'd had a skinful. Luckily I'd got an essay on Foucault with me, so I managed to stay awake.'

'Daddy! Have you brought us a treat?'

'The treat,' Spouse regards his children from beneath half-closed reptilian lids, 'is my presence.'

'Presents? Where?!'

Manage, with difficulty, to convince children they would be happier in the attic than listening to their father revile his few days of liberty in one of the most sparkling Renaissance towns in Britain.

'God knows what they'll find up there,' I observe archly, though no one can appreciate the archness but myself. For the first time for years I find myself thinking: roll on bedtime.

In the event he flings cover back, squints at Marlene's brochure, and cries, 'What the hell's this?'

'Just a little souvenir of your Transatlantic adventure,' I drawl. 'I found it in the attic.' Spouse scrutinises capering tarts with incredulity. 'Don't try and pretend you've never seen it before,' I snap, slightly losing my imperturbable urbanity.

'Don't you take the high moral tone with me, dear,' he retorts. 'What about your Fanny – the only salient characteristic she possesses is the size of her tits.'

Oh, heavens! He is right. Sulk off to sleep, haunted by conviction that I have lost on points and must deflate my heroine in the morning.

thirty-seven

HENRY'S FRIEND JULIAN COMES to tea. Foolishly try to interest children in plateful of beetroot, but they can only see it as an artistic medium.

'Ketchup's better though – can we give ourselves pretend nosebleeds with ketchup, Mum?'

'Certainly not!'

Am persuaded, eventually, to give them tin of spaghetti shaped like characters in TV programme – evidence of cultural degeneration.

After this they run off for *Neighbours*. Wonder how much this resembles home-life of Julian, or whether Lydia provides lots of jolly Athenian games or a table spread with bogrolls and paint from which children assemble scale-model of, say, Nigeria.

Consume whole plateful of beetroot and feel slightly better. Then remember vinegar not good for you so eat half white loaf to mop it up. Then, before intestinal convulsions carry me off, attend to Bonkbuster – or as it might more aptly now be called, Croakbuster. Fanny is still attending her father's deathbed, innocently unaware that I have deftly deflated her bosom without her feeling a thing. Wish someone would do the same for my hips.

Eventually some lines from her favourite poet Guillaume Soutien-Gorge came into her head, and her thin voice rose above the thrumming rain on the roof.

> O Dieu pardonnez-moi
> J'ai le balzac
> Parce que j'ai visité
> La belle Juliette
> Sans porter mon chapeau

Mr Hoddle's eyelids flickered. Fanny leant over him. Was he sinking? Suddenly he reared up on one elbow, his eyes opened, and he squeezed her hand with unusual vigour.

'By heck, lass, I think tha's done t'trick!' he exclaimed. 'Tell thi mother I fancy a morsel o'haslet and a mug o'stout!'

Fanny ran downstairs, and her mother's scream of joy at her news echoed among all the chimneypots of Blunkett Row.

'But, Fanny,' she whispered, 'while tha was with thi feyther, these letters coom for ee.'

Fanny snatched them. One, with its French postmark and rather effete pastel stamp, was evidently from Gertrude. Fanny ripped it open.

'Dearest Fanny!' it read. 'Disaster! I have discovered that M. Boursin has two other mistresses apart from me! Have given in my notice, and am taking the night sleeper for Paris. Oh, meet me at Victoria, at noon on Tuesday the third, I beg – only you can soothe my shattered heart. Gertrude.'

Fanny sighed, hesitated, and threw the strange squared paper on to the fire. Poor Gertrude. What rotters the French were. Apart from Guillaume Soutien-Gorge, of course.

Return to kitchen in search of peppermint tea. Discover sink is blocked, and am forced to crawl into stinking cupboard beneath to investigate.

'Mummee! Henry and Julian've spilt ketchup on the sitting-room carpet!'

'No we haven't! It was her!'

Leap up and crack head violently on something very hard and sharp. Stagger about swearing, at which Harriet looks furious.

'Stop it, Mummy! You're embarrassing me!'

Holding top of head on, lurch out to sitting room and collapse on ketchup-soaked sofa. Bloodstained hank of hair comes away in my hand. Feel faint. Essential I do not die in front of children. They run away upstairs, bored with me and *Neighbours*.

Neighbours! Source of help. Could babysit, ring hospital, call undertaker, etc. But Bernard and Audrey in Madeira and Spouse not expected for another two hours. Grab phone with trembling hands and ring Elaine-over-the-road.

Elaine comes over immediately, tiptoes into sitting room, surveys scene, goes deathly pale, plummets into nearest chair and puts head between knees. It is ten minutes before she feels well enough to drive me to hospital. Honestly, some people. No backbone.

thirty-eight

'REALLY, DULCIE, I HAVEN'T the faintest idea what's going on in his head.'

Elaine is talking about her ex-husband, Marc, who has started telephoning her from Switzerland and making altern-ately seductive and threatening noises. The idea of Swiss threats somehow bizarre, though can easily imagine being cuckooed to death by the clocks.

Feel guilty that I have not got in touch with her for weeks, and make discreet enquiry about her intriguing lodger who resembled Leonard Bernstein, and with whom we once went to the Turkish baths.

'Don't even mention his name or I shall scream!' hisses Elaine. Assure her I cannot remember it anyway, and hope she did not allow him to break her heart.

'Not bloody likely!' Rather regret these references to the sanguine as I am holding a handkerchief to my scalp. 'But, you know, Dulcie, the only thing that keeps me sane sometimes is the thought that you managed it.'

'What?'

'That wonderful lover you had – that plumber chap. At my darkest moments I think, well, Dulcie managed it, so why shouldn't I?'

Astounded at the idea that I could ever be thought to have managed it. Had supposed it was glaringly obvious to everyone that I had mismanaged it.

Arrive at Rusbridge Accident Department. Brace myself for the sight of the groaning and the gory, infinitely worse injured than myself, at the sight of whom I shall faint, just to be a nuisance. However, Accident Dept is empty, apart from friendly woman eager to tap me into her computer.

Cannot remember my NHS number, as usual: can anyone, ever? Wonder why they still bother with NHS numbers. Would be more fun to have NHS names instead. No problem remembering those. Mine would be Hysterix the Gall. Spouse, I suppose, could be Superbowel.

'I've been meaning to go to the doctor, myself,' observes Elaine. 'I can't seem to get my breath, you know. I keep having to do these huge sighs, and then I feel faint.' Instantly realise I cannot get my breath, either, and embark on series of frantic inhalations.

I am seen by various NHS functionaries. Apologise throughout for bothering them, at which they inspect my wound and exclaim Not At All, It's a Nasty Gash – the bastards. There's only one thing worse than your ailments not being taken seriously, and that's your ailments being taken seriously.

End up with shy young radiographer who, avoiding my eye, tells me to undress, put on gown, etc. Always something deeply depressing about this. Institutionalising, I suppose. Induces profound feeling of supine inertia. Although he is too shy to look me in the eye, radiographer, like Webster, can see the skull beneath the skin.

Nice young woman doctor eventually informs me nothing seems to be wrong. Bliss. Joy. But then she spoils it all by handing me a piece of paper which informs the general public of my recent head injury and tells them that 'if severe headache, vomitting [sic], drowsiness or unconsciousness occurs, he/she should be asked to return to Rusbridge Hospital immediately'.

Uncomfortable journey home, because I cannot decide whether to succumb to headache, unconsciousness, breathlessness, or *sic*.

Pick up children from Lydia Rainge-Roughver's where I have a deposit account for emergencies. Lydia enquires tenderly as to my welfare and assures me Henry and Harriet have been angels.

On the way home, however, Harriet snarls: 'I hate Emma and Julian and their house stinks of cat piss.'

Reproach her, though know what she means.

Thank Elaine effusively for driving, support, etc and insist, without conviction, that she must come round to supper sometime. Suddenly her eyes resemble those of a wet dog and she whispers, 'Oh, Dulcie, how kind – I'm so horribly lonely, sometimes I think I'm going mad.'

Suggest she must come to supper next Saturday and rashly assure her we will provide a nice interesting man for her to meet.

thirty-nine

'RIGHT! BEFORE YOU SETTLE down to the football, we're going to make a list of all the eligible men we know.'

Spouse looks startled, nay outraged. Remind him that Elaine is coming to supper next weekend and I have promised her an eligible man to meet.

'How about an illegible man instead?' yawns Spouse. 'I know a few of those.'

'What about Geoffrey?'

Spouse scratches his head, and informs me that his colleague Geoffrey, though matrimonially disengaged, is now madly in love with one of the students.

Staggered by this news, as Geoffrey resembles stout and dyspeptic owl.

'How disgusting,' I sigh, and cross him off the list. Spouse agrees, though I suspect he would secretly fall in love with a student himself if he could find the energy. Am sure several poor girls worship him from afar. Can imagine Spouse presenting rather romantic aspect when glimpsed occasionally across foggy car-park.

Recall my own infatuation, when at Cambridge, with Dr X. Never spoke to him, but faithfully attended his lectures, sitting at the front and admiring the hairs growing out of his nose. Bought his books, copied his handwriting, and regularly came over queer when I glimpsed him in Heffers Bookshop. Said 'Thank you' once to him in University Library when he stood aside to let me out of lift first: heart performed series of vast erratic bounds, rather like rugby ball kicked by Gareth Edwards. Oh, lubricious library! Edifice, despite the pretensions of Athene, secretly consecrated to Aphrodite.

Feel rather cheated that nowadays I seem only able to produce panic by the supermarket till, not passion among the periodicals. Nor indeed are men so worthy of it these days: they have all become slight, dull and round-shouldered – apart from Gordon Brown, of course.

But what of the lone Elaine? Cannot think of any eligible man. All married or gay. Can, however, think of at least five charming, intelligent, eligible women apart from Elaine. Suspect some demographic demon at work here. Probably the Dorothea Brooke syndrome. Recall, with a blush, a certain dream about Michael Foot.

Give up search for eligible man and, after ritual weep at the TV news, prepare for bed. Whilst in bathroom, wonder why a family of four should need seventeen toothbrushes – several resembling Michael Foot at his most windswept. Attempt to throw them away, but hesitate at the thought that they might come in useful, e.g. to clean typewriters, if typewriters ever come back into fashion.

Perhaps, if we cannot dredge up an eligible man for Elaine, she might be prepared to strike up a relationship with a distinguished old toothbrush. Still, knowing my luck, most old toothbrushes probably gay too.

Go to sleep uneasily aware that I must pick up the threads of my Bonkbuster on the morrow. Fanny has resurrected her father by singing French songs at his deathbed, and received news of Gertrude's imminent return, bitter and twisted, from France: betrayed by her Gallic lover. But what of Fanny's Caledonian caresses?

The second envelope was postmarked Auchtereekie, and in a swirling, confident hand. Fanny's fingers trembled as she opened it.

'The memory of our caresses torments me beyond endurance,' wrote the minister, and Fanny's eyeballs vibrated in their sockets as she read. 'I cannot eat, sleep, or deliver a sermon until you return. I roam the hills, pausing only to carve your name on the rocks with my bare fingernails, and thrash my boiling loins with handfuls of thistles –'

There was a knock on the door. Fanny opened it, still blinded and palpitating from Dougal MacPravity's words. A small boy stood out in the rain. He held out an envelope. It was a telegram. Fanny ripped it open, and her heart leapt anew at the message: HECTOR MACRAE FOUND ALIVE STOP ASKING FOR YOU STOP REQUEST YOUR IMMEDIATE RETURN STOP MRS SALMOND STOP.

Spouse suddenly enters with air of successful conjuror.

'I've got Elaine her eligible man,' he beams. 'That plumber johnnie who used to hang around you all the time. Bumped into him outside the post office. Said he'd be delighted.'

forty

To LONDON TO SEE publisher Jeremy D'Arcy, and possibly to buy dress for forthcoming soirée – to which Spouse, in fit of disastrous benevolence, has invited Tom. Of course, Spouse doesn't *know* Tom was my lover – or does he? Is this some kind of fiendish revenge? Lone, lorn Elaine-over-the-road had been promised an eligible man, and this is what Spouse comes up with. If deliberate, quite brilliant on his part. And if not deliberate, quite brilliant on God's – who has got it in for me at the moment.

So why, in the circumstances, a new dress? Well, hell, why not? It's not that I wish to wow Tom anew (tasty anagram lurking there, I suspect). Oh no. Nothing so crass. But I wouldn't mind swanning around looking bewitching whilst Tom heroically devotes himself to poor Elaine. When I say *poor* Elaine, it is to conceal the fact that I am desperately jealous of her svelte form, unmarked by childbirth, and the fact that she is only thirtysomething – unlike self, plunging and soaring seasickly amongst the roaring forties.

However, I fear I shall never swan around looking bewitching again. Although all reference to witchcraft may not have to be abandoned. I would willingly array myself in black rags and a steeple hat if only I could turn people into cold crawly things. Spouse would make a distinguished lizard – no frills. And Tom always was somewhat froglike: slippery, vulnerable and given to sudden reckless leaps.

Attempt to compose mind by reading newspaper. Struck by photograph of Gordon Brown looking for all the world like Dan Dare, Pilot of the Future. But then I suppose that's how Shadow Chancellors think of themselves.

Divert myself for next half-hour by consigning various politicians to their ideal portrait painters. I can see Kenneth Clarke in a Pepysian wig, by Kneller. John Prescott cries out for Holbein's pencil, along with Margaret Beckett, demure in a pearl snood, hands crossed over her prayerbook.

Plenty of candidates on both front benches who could wield pitchforks for Hieronymus Bosch . . . but speaking of Hell, here we are in London.

Jeremy D'Arcy tenderly enquires as to progress of latest Bonkbuster. Assure him that Fanny's bodice has been enthusiastically ripped by both sexes, and that other rippings are looming.

'Who do you see as Fanny if we sell the film rights?' ponders Jeremy. 'How about Patsy Kensit?'

Suggest instead Sylvestre le Touzel, who has already impersonated a Fanny in *Mansfield Park* and would be an even richer source of anagrams.

'And who'd be right for her steaming Scottish lover, the Minister bloke?'

Attempt to conjure up example of steaming Scots actor, but can only think of porridge. Distracted by unsuccessful attempt to create out of Sylvestre le Touzel an anagram about a zealot in the vestry.

Jeremy asks, with strange nervous hesitation, if I have seen the reviews of *Birches*, previous bonkbuster published a few months ago. Oh no, I warble, I'd love to: vilification is so bracing.

Jeremy passes me a file, averting his gaze. Brace myself and jump in bravely, as into freezing lake.

'Vulgar . . . cliché-ridden . . . pure corn . . . pedestrian . . . cheap . . . uninspired . . .'

'What's-his-name liked it,' says Jeremy pityingly. Search, unsuccessfully, for review by What's-his-name, emitting unconvincing gales of laughter the while as new insults leap from the page and stick in my quivering skin.

Towards the end of the torture unearth faintly compliment- ary review from South African paper. Astonished that my books should have penetrated the southern hemisphere, although not sure if entitled to bask in South African plaudits yet. Not sure about buying the oranges either.

Emerge from Jeremy's office feeling like ingrowing porcu- pine and slink off to Paddington entirely oblivious of dress shops.

Once on train, remember that I have also forgotten promised metropolitan delicacy for the children. Never mind. Let them eat humble pie. It runs in the family.

forty-one

'Mum! Isn't Madonna ACE!'

Luckily, this question appears to be rhetorical.

Panic at the thought that Hallowe'en coincides with dinner party to which Spouse has innocently invited Tom. Wonder if Tom still looks as mouthwatering as in the days of yore when he was mine to command. Now, however, he is eligible man destined to be served up to lonely neighbour Elaine, along with roast chicken raised in total freedom in the forests of France. Well, nobody can make a mess of roast chicken, can they?

Harriet has persuaded me to buy a pumpkin. Carve out its innards and thank God I am not an American – would be obliged to concoct a dish therefrom. Instead fling them on compost heap. Painfully reminded that compost heap was started by Tom. He would be pleased at the way it has biodegraded in the months since he was last here. Feel brief pang of envy for compost heap – for which biodegrading appropriate destiny.

Carve out rough features in pumpkin. Somehow resembles Norman Lamont. Insert nightlight, illuminate, switch off kitchen lights, and serve children supper of beans, spuds and bangers (alas not free range). Urge them to bed with promise that Tom will come up and kiss them. Stick chicken in oven, then run upstairs and try on five different dresses, all mysteriously tight. Am obliged to plump for black rippling crêpe trouser-suit with amber silk scarf to hide rippling crêpe neck.

Attempt to distract myself from dread at approaching dinner party by brief foray into Bonkbuster. Heroine Fanny, longing to return to the arms of MacPravity, has just received a wire informing her that Hector Macrae has been found alive. But others also crave her attentions:

Fanny leaned against the doorpost, her breath blooming in the cold Derbyshire twilight. So: her father was alive, Hector Macrae was alive. And as for Dougal MacPravity, she could almost sense the throbs of his heart behind the wild black chaos of his calligraphy. What would Guillaume Soutien-Gorge have said? 'Cette sauce de haute qualité / Est un mélange de fruits orientaux . . .' How true!

The small boy who had delivered the telegram loitered in the dusk. He eyed her balefully.

'An' me sister Vera told me to say,' he announced suddenly, 'as how me Ma's waters has gone and could tha coom reet ower?' Fanny nodded and seized her shawl.

'And . . .' the boy hesitated, bashfully.

'What is it, Albert Heckball?' she asked tenderly. 'Speak up, lad, don't be frit.'

'And . . . can I see thi drawers?' asked the boy, suddenly lewd and bold.

Fanny gave him a thick ear, dived into her clogs, and clattered off to the confinement.

Unendurable tension drives me back to kitchen. Chicken, in Madonnaesque pose, appears to be cooking properly. Spouse is opening bottle of wine. Doorbell rings at which my heart performs sudden manic leap, but it is only Elaine. She looks horribly attractive and tactlessly young. Aware of need to warn her that eligible man is Tom, whom she will recognise as my erstwhile lover, but Spouse appears, preventing my explanation.

Ten minutes later, the doorbell rings again. Leap to answer it, though halfway there realise it would have been better to let Spouse go, giving me time for brief briefing of Elaine. Compose heart: it was all over a year ago, at my instigation. Remind myself urgently of Tom's callowness, naïveté, spaniel eyes and taste for Tarot and Nostradamus. Mentally stiffen my skin into chainmail and fling open door. Tom stands there grinning, his hair bespangled with raindrops.

'Hi,' he whispers puckishly, 'trick or treat?'

forty-two

TOM, SPOUSE, ELAINE AND self poised to devour chicken. Bizarre event. Tom seems completely relaxed – the bastard – and beams at me serenely as one might salute favourite old aunt. Elaine unsure at first whether she was allowed to fascinate my ex-lover under my nose, and in the presence of my uncharacteristically genial Spouse, but three glasses of Muscadet appear to have swept away her misgivings and she is now flirting heroically in stereo.

Whilst lifting chicken out of oven I hear Tom say that *The Rocky Horror Show* is on in Bristol. Oh, cries Elaine, I've always wanted to see that. Chicken performs sudden leap and spatters my rippling crêpe trouser-suit with hot fat. Crêpe cringes as if wounded like particularly upsetting sequence from *Life on Earth*. Utter tiny self-deprecating scream and beg to be excused so that I may sponge my singed thighs.

Wonder if the memory of my hot thighs will distract Tom from *The Rocky Horror Show*, but as I go upstairs I hear him promising to ring theatre, get tickets, etc, and Spouse assuring him that he and I won't want to come as we saw it the first time around when we were young.

Discard fat-spattered trousers and search in vain for garment which will make me look twenty-eight and optimistic – or, failing that, invisible. Everything suddenly dirty or too tight. Settle eventually for very old kaftan within which I lurk like vulnerable New Age traveller in wigwam fearing force nine gale.

'Good God!' exclaims Spouse when I reappear. 'What the hell's that?'

'Oh, it's lovely!' cries Elaine unconvincingly, and Tom produces unpleasant smirk. Long to kill them all, preferably with kaftan, but succeed only in dipping both sleeves in gravy.

Chicken is overcooked and falls to bits, but company distracted by Elaine, who though normally rather quiet and tense, exhibits rare fit of hilarity under the influence of Bacchus.

Decide that I do genuinely hope that Tom and Elaine hit it off. True, the first moment of beholding Tom on my doorstep again was something of a blow to the solar plexus, but once he gets on to Nostradamus I breathe more easily. And after Nostradamus, the mystic East.

'Yeah, and in the summer I went to India and it was, just, well, overwhelming, y'know?'

'Oh, I've always wanted to go to India!' shrieks Elaine. For a moment I fear that Tom will offer to book the tickets tomorrow.

'Yeah, you must, there's this guy living in a cave, he's been there for fifty years or something, and he just lives on roots and leaves and stuff and y'know, meditates all day.'

'I've been thinking of becoming a vegetarian,' sighs Elaine, at which we all gaze guiltily at the chicken bones and wish it was still running joyfully about in the forests of France.

It seems to me that Elaine is more haunted by good intentions than anyone else I have met. The road to hell, etc, etc. For a brief moment enjoy feeling of complacency that I have myself managed to discard several good intentions, nay, replaced them with evil ones. But I expect that road leads to hell, too. They all seem to, these days.

After the rigours of the dinner party, my heroine's obstetric duties seem almost humdrum.

Several hours later, with twins safely delivered, Fanny walked numbly home. The memory of the newborns' innocent faces lit up her brain. Clarence and Percy Heckball. How soon would it be before they were translated from flawless cherubs to lewd little boys? Was human nature irrevocably soiled? And how soon could she get back to the arms of the minister? Or to Mr Macrae's . . . Fanny blushed at the bold chaos of her thoughts. And yet if it proved her duty to caress the dear headmaster back to health, who was she to hesitate?

forty-three

'ARE YOU *SURE* YOU don't mind, Dulcie?'

Elaine-over-the-road is over-the-moon: outing to theatre with Tom was, by all accounts, a roaring success.

'Of course not! Tom and I are Ancient History. I'll be delighted if you two hit it off.'

Show teeth in approximation of gracious smile.

'Well, I don't know, but . . .' Elaine's hands are trembling. 'We're going out again this Saturday – if you're sure you don't mind?'

'For God's sake, Elaine! How many times do I have to tell you? I'm *delighted*!'

Money back if not benighted.

Afterwards, whilst cutting up cereal boxes with Harriet, think perhaps I really ought to be delighted. What is one to do, after all, with old lovers? One cannot cut them up and make a boat for the Sindies out of them.

'And can we make whores, Mummy?'

'What?'

'Whores – to row with.'

'Oars – oh, yes. We can use Grandma's old knitting needles.'

Soon the Sindies are sailing across the kitchen table, vacuous grins and pert bosoms akimbo, in search of lonely eight-inch sailor boys.

Wonder about origin of akimbo. Suspect it is part of the debris of colonialism. In the Victorian era, of course, ex-lovers could go off and become sailors or colonial administrators. No Navy and no Empire nowadays, alas. Briefly entertained by thought of Tom, in topi, circa 1920s, listening enraptured to guru in cave. One does so want one's ex-lovers to find a good home; lead purposeful, interesting, although of course tragically shadowed lives.

'Mummee! How long is it till Christmas?'

Heave deep sigh. Advent season seems sometimes like epic bout of pre-menstrual tension. Experience deep urge to escape, perhaps to Indian cave. Oh for a land where religious festivals might revolve around emptiness.

Henry bursts in bearing toy catalogue tactlessly lent by Mrs Body.

'Mum! Can I have a Himalaya Pro Mountain Bike? Please, Mum!'

'Certainly not! There aren't any mountains within miles of Rusbridge, anyway.'

Have never quite understood the point of mountain bikes, even though they have been mentioned on *The Archers*: a sure sign of assimilation within mainstream society. Given a mountain, I would gladly gaze upon it in the manner recommended by Wordsworth; even, if absolutely unavoidable, walk up the first 200 feet of it, but ride a bicycle up it? The idea bears all the hallmarks of *homo* at his most *sapiens*.

Harriet grabs catalogue and demands a Ker-plunk, a Giggle Wiggle or a Whack Attack. Warn that if children do not shut up and go away, a Whack Attack all too likely.

Wonder, in resulting lull, whether Tom ever thinks of me at all, and if so, with how much vehemence.

As she turned into Blunkett Row, a figure loomed up out of the gloom. Fanny flinched and gasped as the man seized her sleeve.

'You have forgotten me, Fanny Hoddle!' he whispered urgently. 'But not an hour has passed of your long Caledonian absence when I have not recalled your every feature with a feverishness, my dear girl, which has quite burned my soul to a crisp! Come to my studio tonight, no, tomorrow – the light will be better – and let my little stick of charcoal pay just tribute to your pulchritude!'

In the wan lamplight Fanny recognised the face of Melvyn Potter, the artist in oils, chalks and watercolours, who had spied upon her and Gertrude as they bathed in Rough Dike Reservoir. To think that the hapless Potter had intrigued her once! Now she had felt the hot breath of a minister of the Church of Scotland upon her naked clavicles, the temptations of Potter's studio were limp indeed. How dare he waylay her here, on her own doorstep!

'Cleck off, dingbat!' she hissed, and dealt him a devastating blow with her knee. 'I belong to the Church!' And with a magnificent toss of the head, she was gone.

forty-four

Potter sobbed wetly on to the cobbles. The Venus of Berpsover had spurned him, as he had suspected she would. Never mind. He would

stagger home and console himself with Rowlandson's Erotic
Engravings – *and on the morrow, when he had recovered . . . there
was always Vera Heckball.*

  Fanny slipped into her little truckle bed and reached for her copy of
Paradise Lost. *The candlelight clothed her naked limbs in gold, for
Fanny felt too hot, tonight, for nightdress or bedclothes. Trembling,
her fingers found the place in the text and eagerly her large quivering
eyeballs adjusted to the print. She was impatient to enjoy another half
an hour of Satan.*

Must whisk Fanny back over the border to the arms of her
amorous minister. But perhaps that is too modest a destiny.
There are, after all, royal castles in Scotland. I can see her now,
fainting decoratively in the capable arms of a prince, outlined
against the blazing battlements . . . a classic of its time: *Gone
with the Windsors.*

  'Mummee! There was a comdom in the girls' toilets at
school today.'

  'What's a comdom?'

  'Don't you know?' Harriet simpers. 'It's . . . men put them
on their peonies to collect the seeds.'

  Wonder if this horticultural convenience would make a
good Christmas present for Aunt Elspeth.

  Receive invitation to subscribe to *The Economist.* Invitation
makes rather robust assumptions about my lifestyle.

A colleague turns to you at a management meeting and asks
if you understand the implications of the GATT negoti-
ations. *What can you say?* Your father-in-law wants to know
if he should invest in privatised British coal? *What do you
think?* One of your competitors is opening up in El
Salvador. *What's going on?* . . . It's not easy to keep abreast
of events, it's just vital. Because without a clear, informed
view of the world you work in, you can rely on nothing but
that age-old affliction: gut feeling.

How dare *The Economist* stigmatise gut feeling? Have
always been irritated by people with clear, informed views.
Smug bastards. Give me guts any day. Am particularly
charmed, however, by the thought of one of my competitors
opening up in El Salvador. Wonder, albeit idly, where exactly
El Salvador is. Perhaps subscription would make a good
Christmas present for Spouse, though: place form in In-tray.

Obscurely pleased that, though I do not aspire to competitors, I do at least have an In-tray. Then suddenly, gut feeling rears its ugly head and informs me that I do have a competitor: Elaine, who has transcended her former lowly identity as mere neighbour and is actively consorting with my ex-lover Tom.

Nonsense, I inform gut feeling. I do not see other women as rivals. It was All Over with Tom aeons ago: I was repeatedly urged to elope with him and decided against it, displaying both sagacity and restraint. *The Economist* would have been proud of me. Good luck to Tom and Elaine; were they to sail off into the sunsets of El Salvador together, I would wish them Godspeed and return to my lofty perusal of GATT.

Oh heck. Supper looms, and the cupboard is as bare as a female competitor in *Come Dancing*. Seize children and propel towards supermarket, as Spouse is out, probably at a faculty meeting. He has management meetings and colleagues; I rejoice in kids and carrier bags.

'Mum! Can we have Pop-tarts? Can we have Monster Munches?'

Accede instantly to every demand as have no stomach for a fight today.

In fact, halfway down third aisle, become aware that stomach is simmering unpleasantly. Am going to be sick! In public! Heart leaps into overdrive; ears flutter; knees knock. Abandon half-full trolley, seize children and push, pale and sweating, through thronged checkout. Dash into loo where am not sick after all. Lean quivering against wall.

'Never do that again, Mummy!' Harriet hisses, mortified.

Perhaps *The Economist* was right after all about gut feeling being an affliction. Sheepishly resume shopping, though when halfway home, realise with panic that have forgotten loo paper for third time this week. Wonder if *The Economist* is absorbent as well as absorbing.

forty-five

Alice rings to convey season's greetings a few days early as she and Saskia are jetting off to St Lucia for the duration. Sigh anew that Fate did not make me a lesbian, loading me instead with horrendous burden of Yuletide labours for indifferent family. Also complain that my erstwhile lover Tom is now consorting with Elaine-over-the-road, indeed that I must face Drinks at Elaine's on Boxing Day.

'It's no use crying over spilt milk, Dulcie!' snaps Alice briskly. 'You told me once he was so horribly spanielly, it made you want to scream.'

'And I've started having panic attacks in supermarkets.'

'Well, that's just the human condition.'

'And I haven't bought a single candle yet.'

'Who needs candles? What's wrong with electricity? It's all so bloody *medieval*.'

Complain further about medieval duties awaiting me – a sort of Norman Lament – before Alice rings off, pretending to hear the taxi that is to whisk her westwards.

Feel that Alice was rather hard on candles; probably for feminist reasons. Am increasingly beguiled by candlelight, myself. Makes us all look like Titians. Unlike fluorescent tube, which makes us all look like Lucian Freuds.

Henry comes in smirking confidentially and whispers that Harriet asked him if Santa was real and that he insisted yes, he was, and does that mean he has earned an extra 50p?

'I didn't say 50p *every* time you mentioned it!' I hiss. Harriet runs in.

'What's all that about 50p? I want 50p too!' she bawls.

Inform her that no one has 50p, not even me, and I have heard quite enough about what she wants to last me well into 1993.

Amazed at Harriet's ability to believe in Santa after three years at school. But then, what the human race contrives to believe in beggars, if not buggers, the imagination.

Market forces, for example: though Chris Patten only has to show his teeth for the Shag Hen Index to plummet into the void. Family values, that's another, though personally have concluded that the family is an instrument for the enslavement of women and I would lead a more rewarding life in Holloway. Serbia, psychoanalysis, Royal Jelly: if folk believe in these, why not in Santa?

Would not like the idea of Santa zealots, however. Can imagine it all getting out of hand and bands of hysterical young Santanistas, heavily disguised in cotton wool, roaming the streets with kalashnikovs looking for Scrooges and agnostics.

Spouse enters, tragically fatigued, and warns me that there are some carol singers working their way up Cranford Gardens, dressed up as medieval minstrels. Appalled at this news, as carol singers always somehow excruciatingly embarrassing even when only in duffel coats. Groan and shudder, symptoms which Spouse rather unsympathetically identifies as signs of pre-minstrel tension.

Prepare 50p piece, as sole relic of good old proper money when small change weighed down one's pockets and a single monstrous penny could derail the Edinburgh express. Put kettle on (comforting ritual) and smile obediently when Spouse reads me account from *Rusbridge Gazette* of a Santa sacked for inebriation. Blotto in the Grotto. Distracted by tendency of kettle to make noise like machine-gun when getting warm, unlike picturesque whistling song as in medieval days of yore.

Gone, too, is the merry clink of milk bottle: replaced, *chez nous*, by the silent convenience of cardboard. Although convenience is perhaps not the right word. Vow that this time I shall successfully Pull Back Wings to Form Spout, but alas! – edge is ragged and torn as usual and milk leaps out in stereo to right and left, missing mug entirely and flooding table.

Disregard Alice's proverbial advice about spilt milk, and burst into tears, at the very moment when strains of 'Hark the Herald' drift across from the Twills' porch next door. Spouse looks surprised. Attribute tears to festive season.

'Ah well,' observes Spouse sardonically, 'it'll all be over by Christmas.'

forty-six

DRINKS AT ELAINE'S AT 6 p.m. Prevail upon Tracey Body to babysit for necessary one and a half hours, though she asks if she may bring Pigs. Startled by this request, but it turns out to be her boyfriend's nickname. Hope that Tracey will not do anything unfortunate with Pigs in front of the children.

Anxiety about children, however, completely eclipsed by anticipatory twinges at the thought that I am about to be confronted by Tom in his new role as Elaine's . . . well, not sure what. Squire, perhaps? Hope they will not be tactless enough to canoodle in front of me. Not confident about my ability to preserve relaxed demeanour if they canoodle in front of me in front of Spouse. In front of God, too, to extend the hierarchy.

If God, or indeed gods, do observe our human actions, rather like divine couch-potatoes flicking through endless satellite TV channels, whatever must they make of our apparently increasing tendency to persecute and kill one another in their names? But I suppose some gods would lap up that sort of thing.

'Do you think God exists?' I ask Spouse, hoping he has not noticed that I am busily discarding third choice of dress and settling for the sexless safety of the trouser-suit. Luckily he is engaged in the tricky operation of trimming the hairs which have started to grow out of his ears. 'I mean, is there life after death, do you think?'

'Is there life before death, that's what I'm worried about,' retorts Spouse. 'And where the hell's my comb? Have you stolen it again?'

Arrive at Elaine's to find a whole field of folk but brain instantly informs me that Tom is over by the curtains, attending to the music with unpleasantly proprietorial air. Vow that I will not look at him till absolutely unavoidable – at least for the first half-hour. He straightens up and instantly our eyes meet with deafening crash. Under the scorching laser of his gaze, my spleen boils and steam comes screaming out of my navel.

Attempt a smile, but it twitches manically like a windscreen wiper on the blink. Tom does not bother with such trivia, producing instead the kind of glowering pout I have only previously seen in coffee ads on TV. Drag my eyes away with what I am sure must be audible ripping sound, and congratulate Elaine on the piquancy of her mulled wine.

'Watch out, Dulcie, it's a killer,' she warns, but I am distracted from her words by her luminously sexy appearance. Though as slim and gleaming as an eel, she has nevertheless also been blessed with a cleavage and is displaying it – judiciously and tastefully, of course. Sigh at the thought that my own figure is daily approximating to that of Bill Beaumont, although fear I shall never attain Bill's majestic bosom.

Am introduced to small man with halitosis who seems to want to talk about the recession. Attempt to stop him at all costs and recklessly steer the conversation towards Royalty. Small man declares himself a Republican and finds the whole thing a tasteless charade.

Suddenly feel my kidney caressed and warm breath on my neck. Thrills zip up and down my sciatic nerves until I realise it is only Spouse, asking uxoriously for the name or phone number of the printer who does our headed notepaper. Provide necessary details and become aware that Tom is watching us, though manage, thank God, not to catch his eye.

Elaine replenishes my glass. Request, rather loudly, that she must not do so again or I shall disgrace myself. Small man is patiently awaiting his moment to introduce me to a whole paragraph of malodorous statistics. Listen with head cocked to simulate intelligence, though secretly trying to overhear Tom's conversation with statuesque blonde. Drain glass to dregs but recession still boring and Tom still inaudible.

Elaine offers Tom the peanuts. Attempt, whilst nodding at small man, to discern whether Tom is looking down her cleavage or not. Accept more wine. Tom disappears. Small man starts talking about the Small Businessman and wonder if he is one himself. Suddenly receive peanut-flavoured whisper in left ear: 'We've got to stop meeting like this.' Turn, but he is gone. Room tilts slightly and for a moment have hallucination that we are all aboard ocean liner, and sinking. Ask small man whether he thinks human life is a random cosmic accident.

'Or are we,' I muse, suddenly *fortissimo* (strong stuff that mulled wine), 'a mere virus in the lap-top of the gods?'

Small man makes an excuse and leaves.

forty-seven

HOME ALONE FOR NEW Year as usual, because Spouse takes the children to Kirkwhinnie for Hogmanay with Great Aunt Elspeth. He uses this modest excursion to pump up his martyrdom for weeks before and afterwards. Still, my memories of Aunt Elspeth's hospitality suggest that perhaps he is entitled to a little self-conscious heroism. Her cakes, for example, if fired from cannon, could destroy castles.

But to my task: I must reunite the heroine of my Bonk-buster with her Caledonian minister, whose Calvinist combinations are crackling in anticipation of her return. But I sit abstracted before my word-processor, lost in dreams of previous Hogmanays when Spouse's absence facilitated dalliance with Tom. Now, alas, it is Elaine to whose arms he flies. Never mind. I shall lose myself in my work.

'Fanny!' panted Dougal MacPravity, the veins in his neck throbbing visibly against his clerical collar, 'your absence has been a torment to me!' And he crushed her to his hot habit.

Ecclesiastical rogering comes up against the tiresome complications of garb. What do ministers of the Church of Scotland wear? And what do they wear *under that*? But wait! The muse assists . . .

It was dark up here on the slopes of Auld MacNookie. The moonlight threw MacPravity's majestic brow into stark relief, and the wild wind tossed his black locks hither and thither. Fanny felt herself melt in his arms, as they threw themselves recklessly down on to a bed of springy heather – fit nuptial couch, thought Fanny, for a Scottish Titania. Soon he had flung his garments off, and knelt above her, reminding her of the photographic plates of Michelangelo's David, which Gertrude had shown her during their sessions on Renaissance Art. Only a lot hairier.

'Come, my love,' he muttered, savage but somehow tender, lowering his –

At this promising moment, however, the phone rings. Mine, not theirs. Fanny and Dougal had the infinite good fortune to be born before mobile phones. Grab receiver with bad grace and grumpily identify myself.

'Dulcie? This is Tom. I was wondering if you'd like to come round tomorrow. Just for tea, you know.'

'I – I – I – I – well, what a good idea! Er – is it a party?'
Lament that my answer fell short of perfect sang-froid.
'Oh no. I just thought it would be nice to see you.'

'Well . . . well, yes. It would. Be nice to see you.'

He proposes 4 p.m. and rings off, leaving me thrashing about in perturbation. Walk up and down wringing my hands like someone in 1930s melodrama. What does he mean by it? Is he uncontrollably seized by a resurgence of passion? Come to think of it, am I? Will he grab me and press me to his hot habit?

Coast is clear, i.e. Spouse's return scheduled for four days hence. But what about Elaine, potential bosom chum? Will my visit to Tom's be a dreadful betrayal of female solidarity? Bloody well hope so! Sod Elaine. I saw him first.

Return to word-processor, but cannot concentrate. Suppose he only wants to establish new, friendly Platonic entente? Blood runs cold. Suppose he is going to issue new series of ultimata about elopement? Blood runs even colder. Wonder what on earth I am hoping for. Hurl myself wilfully back into Bonkbuster, and describe hillside coupling in the sort of lewd detail which will lead, we hope, to big bucks.

Afterwards, Fanny laid her head on his massive chest. She felt a sublime calm. But her lover was strangely restless.

'Och, forgive me, Lord!' he groaned. 'For I have sinned!'

Fanny glanced angrily upwards, but her indignation was interrupted by a strange smoky smell. She sniffed the air. Hardacre's Thick Old Shag! She sat up wildly and stared into the darkness. Gertrude! Could it be?

Phone rings again. Run to it expecting Tom again, somehow: foolish. But it is Elaine.

'Could I come over and have a chat, Dulcie? Would you mind? Only, things are getting . . . a bit strange.'

You're telling me.

forty-eight

'HE'S BEHAVING REALLY ODDLY, Dulcie.' Elaine cradles cup of tea with shaking hand. Suspect I may soon be required to offer absorbent shoulder to console her for eccentricities of my erstwhile lover. 'He said he'd ring, but . . . Still, I suppose he might be away.'

Agree, though uncomfortably aware that not half an hour ago Tom rang me up and issued invitation for tomorrow. Can it be that he does not find Elaine so very attractive after all, despite her svelte youth? Can it be that, like other great men of our time, he prefers women who remind him of his granny? Shake head and tut-tut in elderly way, though assuring her that he often disappears without explanation, and that the conjunction of plumbing with Christmas might well have proved disastrous.

'The thing is, Dulcie, did you find him a bit . . . well . . .' Elaine hesitates tantalisingly, the hint of a grimace playing over her lovely lips. What? Has he alienated her so soon? Something to do with health food perhaps? Or has Nostradamus reared his ugly head? '. . . a bit slow?'

'Slow?'

'S-sexually. I mean, we've not really ever . . . you know.'

Attempt to pull expression of sympathetic outrage over face, but it feels like jumper that has shrunk in the wash. Shake head doubtfully, as if suggesting I cannot really remember much about Tom's love life with me, at all. Try hard to suppress memories of many a hasty bout of panting in a series of unpromising venues. Huge surge of beastly triumph attempts to unfurl within me, but beat it back and instead dredge up a few miserable squits of feminine fellow-feeling.

'You poor thing!'

At this meagre consolation, Elaine bursts into tears and I propel her towards my shoulder – a manoeuvre difficult to achieve when protagonists are sitting in adjoining armchairs. Seriously rick my back, and a deep groan suggests that Elaine may also have ricked hers. Try not to conjecture whether, in precisely twenty-four hours' time, Tom and I may be locked in altogether more satisfying embrace.

Phone rings. Extricate myself with apologies and hope it will not be Tom cancelling tomorrow. Elaine starts to blow nose with a raucous abandon for one so elegant. I lift the receiver and am informed by a Caledonian voice that she has a call for me from Kirkwhinnie. It is Spouse.

'Harriet's a bit off-colour so I think we'll come back overnight,' he sighs. 'Be with you shortly after breakfast, probably.'

Have time for a brief pang of anguish that my tryst with Tom has withered i'the bud, then make urgent enquiries about Harriet's health.

Spouse assures me she is all right. Suspect he is exaggerating her symptoms in order to escape early from Aunt Elspeth's. Have oft done same myself. Though recall was trumped many times by Aunt Elspeth producing even worse symptoms in order to keep us there. Spouse asks what is that noise in the background, it sounds like a wild boar rooting for truffles. Inform him it is Elaine blowing her nose.

Inform Elaine family is returning early, at which she produces entirely unwelcome burst of envy for my lovely husband and children.

'I'm so lonely, Dulcie, it's awful!' she shudders. Invite her to stay the night in Henry's bed, though it is covered with plastic paratroopers. She accepts eagerly, and supposes it is as near to having a toyboy as she will ever get.

Wonder if early return of family is divine retribution for my failure to sympathise. Endeavour to make up for it by enduring her subsequent two hours of lamentation without even once glancing at my watch.

Stay up late to titivate Bonkbuster before children arrive to renew my enslavement.

Fanny stilled the groaning minister with an impetuous gesture. The smell of Hardacre's Thick Old Shag still hung on the air.

'Gertrude . . .?' called Fanny softly. The bracken rustled in the dark.

'Oh, Fanny!' came the familiar low voice, choked with sobs. 'How could you? You did not meet me at Victoria. I see my hopes for a reconciliation are in vain. No matter. I shall distract my poor broken heart by travel. I have always wanted to visit Eastern Bulimia.' And she was gone, leaving only a glowing cigarette butt, which, like a symbol of their spent passion, flared briefly in the stillness and was extinguished.

forty-nine

SPOUSE RETURNS EARLY FROM Kirkwhinnie with semi-sick children, so I must decline tantalising invite to tea with erstwhile lover Tom. Strangely relieved, when I ring him to bow out, to find myself conversing only with his answerphone. My hackles twitch at his outgoing message: 'Yah um, sorry, can't actually talk to you right now, so why don't you, like, stick a message on here after the toot. Cheers.'

Can it be that I was seriously in love with this person? Still, must be charitable. No one's at their best on their outgoing message.

'Mummeeee!' Children fasten themselves to me like ticks latching on to a blowsy old sow. Or do ticks prefer fur? Stagger under the burden of their love, and fall on top of them, to their evident delight. Mem.: must try to ensure that there is always a pair of squashy children to break one's fall. Spouse throws himself into armchair with air of man who has fought off a global threat to civilisation single-handed.

Aunt Elspeth's gift to Spouse was a stuffed owl much resembling Lord Howe, which I place on the sideboard next to the British Museum replica of the god Eros, who resembles David Gower. Harriet demands I also admire Shivering Dolly given to her by Aunt Elspeth. Whatever will dolls do next? She talks, she cries, she wets her nappy, she shivers . . .

'And, in the case of Sindy, she sins,' suggests Spouse.

'Or she could fart!' shouts Henry. 'Then she could be Windy.' He then loudly demonstrates his own prowess in the Aeolian arts.

I express the hope they both behaved in front of Aunt Elspeth. Spouse informs me later that the only sticky moment was when provoked by something on TV, Harriet demanded, 'Daddy, what's an orgasm?' over the oatcakes.

Somehow this reminds me that my Bonkbuster needs urgent attention, so, once children are in bed, reunited with their plastic playmates and dinky instruments of war, I leave Spouse to alcoholic contemplation of TV sports and seek my study. Stuck with plot, so resort as usual to plagiarism of *The Archers*.

Fanny contemplated the letter: on thick ecclesiastical paper, Dougal MacPravity offered her his hand in marriage, which he felt alone could consecrate the passion they had so unfortunately celebrated on the scree-scattered slopes of Auld MacNookie. Only within the sacrament, he assured her, could he permit himself those joys which were otherwise unpleasing in the sight of God.

Fanny glanced upwards, but there was no divine gaze, only Mrs Salmond's rather cracked plaster. Did she wish to be a minister's wife? She had thought, at times, she might have been happier in the more secular company of dear Hector Macrae, the headmaster, but since his mishap with the landslip he had been so jealously guarded by his sister Mairi that even Fanny's blameless little sago puddings had been refused audience with him.

'Dinna take it ill,' Mairi had insisted between tight lips, 'but he's unco guid a pawkie sollas mae uister arken whee holler.'

'Of course,' Fanny had mumbled, backing away from the alien northern dialect, and clutching her two despised little sago puddings with a fierce protectiveness. (She had shared them later, with Mrs Salmond, over a smoky peat fire.)

Fanny would not have minded marrying the minister, but for her instinct that she would always feel that God was in bed with them. Nor, she was sure, would she ever be at home here. She did not even speak the language. Indeed, after Gertrude's tuition, she would be better understood in France. From Gaelic to Garlic.

Gertrude! Her heart gave a sudden lurch. Gertrude had embarked on an epic journey towards Bulimia, and would even now be setting foot in the flat but history-saturated fields of Flanders. Fanny had always fancied Flanders. Not to mention the alpine slopes of Mirren, the ruined palaces of Thermos, the bustling Levantine port of Sozij. She was seized by a violent desire to –

Suddenly word-processor goes dark, as does whole of creation, and all the domestic machines die in unison with an exhalation of ticks and groans. Am I dead? If so, am certainly still seated on chair of cheap commercial design which hardly does credit to the Afterlife.

'It's a power cut!' cries Spouse far away. Grope gingerly towards him, but instead endure appalling encounter with stuffed owl.

fifty

'WHERE THE HELL ARE the candles?'

Spouse manages to use seasonal power cut as evidence of my domestic negligence. Suddenly tempted, instead of calling out helpful reply, to keep mum and lurk menacingly in the dark. Wonder how soon he would lose his nerve and beg me to reveal myself, rather like votive priest addressing capricious goddess.

Capricious goddess would certainly be healthy role model. Why should I be expected to have bought candles for just such an emergency as this? Why should my weary hand be ever ready to soothe, to scrub, to sweep, to set a-simmer nourishing soups for my beloved ones? Why not instead smite the bastards into pillars of amethyst with one flash of my divine eye?

Ouch! Sod it! Smite instead shin on mysterious, but malevolent, piece of furniture.

'The candles are in the drawer of the kitchen table.'

'I didn't know there *was* a drawer in the kitchen table.'

I shouldn't boast about that one, my Lord, unless you're wearing your smiteproof weskit. Strange things happen in the dark.

But of course I avert my wild yellow eyes, draw in my fangs and instead equip him with candles, indeed with Lumogaz camping lamp. I helpfully read the instructions by candlelight in fourteen languages (my favourite is Finnish: *Aseta hehku-sukka polttimen paalle suureman suun ollessa* . . . have the Finns all got double vision?). But Spouse ignores my polyglot advice and ignites it wrongly, ruining the mantle. Luckily with my divine prescience I have foreseen this and offer him two spares.

Eventually a seventeenth-century glow springs up, and the kitchen resembles a Caravaggio, but for lamentable absence of beautiful young men with long eyelashes. Suddenly remember having candlelit bath with Spouse in Oxford aeons ago: when he still had eyelashes. Long before he was fatally eSpoused, in fact. I think we were even drinking champagne. It glimmers archaeologically in my memory, a relic of some Mycenaean age.

'Mummmmaaaaaaagh!'

Banshee shriek from above informs me that Harriet has awoken and not been reassured as usual by the friendly twinkle of her electric nightlight, a luminous mushroom inhabited by two insanely cheerful maggots.

Race upstairs with candle (a mistake: hot red wax all over back of hand). Kneel by bedside.

'There, there, darling. Want a pee? Come on, then. Mummy will take you. The electricity's off, it's all right.'

Grab child, slither along landing wall, and locate bathroom, but Harriet is not reassured. She stares in panic at my red wax stigmata, my sinister candle and even more sinister expression of tenderness and cries out: 'No, Mummy! Don't go sideways!'

Not sure if this a reasonable request, given de Bono's thesis on the fruitfulness of the lateral, but assure her it was a momentary lapse and I will never go sideways again. Feel her brow: it is burning. Whilst peeing, she gives me a fearful look and requests Daddy.

As I am wiping her bottom by candlelight (*pace* Flemish domestic scene, *circa* 1680, Cornelius van Klootsak), the phone rings. A crash and a curse downstairs suggest that Spouse has knocked over something priceless (well, by our standards) in an attempt to find phone. A male rational daylight soul is his, of course, unlike Yours Truly Queen of the Night. His voice echoes ghostily up the shadowed stairs.

'Tom who?'

Terror leaps into eye, heart, etc. Propel daughter back to bed, kiss her and depart – backwards, to be reassuring.

'It's for you!'

Lurch towards stairs, but in the dark trip on one of Henry's plastic Cruise missiles and fall headlong, with loud caco-phony, down into hall. Past life does not flash before my eyes – only the desperate awareness that we have just run out of bogpaper and therefore dying at this moment is doubly an act of domestic negligence.

Sit up at bottom of stairs and try to focus on the two Spouses hovering above me. They enquire if I am all right.

'I can see double.'

Wonder if, now I can see double, it means I have been translated into Finnish. If not altogether finished. Hope not. Feel bruised pang of fellow-feeling with other fallers: Amy

Robsart, Satan, Adam, etc, but have no desire to meet them quite yet.

fifty-one

Act now, Mrs D. Domum, and you can have it all! Thus does TIME *International Magazine* promise me endless riches in the Million Dollar Sweepstakes. All I have to do is peel off stickers and stick them in the correct boxes on the entry form, thus *Activating* my *Eligibility*. However, am still recovering from recent fall downstairs and doubt whether I could have my eligibility activated without serious discomfort.

Stiff all over, except in morale, of course, I languish on sofa and am waited on by Mrs Body, who brings me cups of tarry PG Tips and urges me not to stir from sofa too soon as falls can be nasty things. Henry and Harriet have returned to school, Spouse to his lectures, leaving me leisure in which to ponder unrepeatable offers. Close scrutiny of the document, however, convinces me that I would be unable to cope even with Third Prize.

'*Your choice of $10,000 worth of electronics: VCR, CD Changer, Speakers, Turntable, Camcorder – you name it!*' Am barely able to imagine what a VCR or a CD Changer might be, and had I indeed been given the chance to name the whole lot, they would rejoice in something much more colourful and expansive than VCR and CD. Would prefer old man with hurdy-gurdy to almost any electronic sound system, but then, have oft thought I was born 100 years too late. Perhaps this is why I earn my living by plunging picturesquely into the past.

Speaking of which, Bonkbuster is poised at a critical moment, as my dear Fanny hesitates between the joys of a Calvinist marriage and a mind- and body-boggling journey across Europe. Seize pen and exercise book. Have always fancied the picaresque.

'*Dear Dougal,*' Fanny wrote in a trembling hand, '*Alas I cannot accept your kind offer of Matrimony. My friend and teacher Miss Gertrude Lillywhite always warned me against it as the tomb of the wild female spirit – how did she put it? "The broad inviting road to* the bourgeois and the banal." Dearest Dougal, I wish you every happiness in your future life, and rejoice in the thought that, should these words cause you any distress, you will be amply comforted by your beloved Maker.'

She signed the letter *Ever Your Contrite Fanny*, thrust it into one of Mrs Salmond's thick wholemeal envelopes, ran downstairs and gave it to the dear lady, who was weeping over Fanny's ironing.

'Och, I shall miss ye wheek a curdie!' she lamented, smoothing one of Fanny's worn bustbodices with her gnarled old fingers. 'Ye've been like a daughter to me, ye braw wee beastie! I'll pack ye a basin o'me oatmeal pudden for the morrow, an' a morsel o'pickled Capercaillie's hurdies.' Fanny thanked the good soul ardently, and many a tear they shed upon each other's tippets.

'Only think, Mrs Salmond,' cried Fanny at length, drawing away from her hostess, an eager smile shining through her tears, 'of my adventure! Travelling across Europe, and be sure I shall send you – oh, such exotic Cartes Postales! And when I return to these shores again, after visiting my dear parents in Berpsover, it is to your hearth that I shall fly, to tell you of my travels and taste once again the ambrosia of your porridge.'

'Och aye, gae ballaknockie uidshagger!' lamented Mrs Salmond, toppled by extreme emotion into what Fanny supposed was her native Gaelic. 'There's just the little matter o'three shilling and fourpence halfpenny, now, dear, for th'balance o'th'rent.'

Wonder what Mrs Body is doing upstairs. Hope she is not taking advantage of my temporary convalescence by going through my drawers. Thank God I threw Tom's letters away in Herefordshire, eighteen months ago – though I have since learned that the SAS has their headquarters there. Perhaps the pertinent details of my peccadillo are already entered on to some all-knowing computer in a bunker a hundred feet below Ocle Pychard. Perhaps eventually TIME Life International or the *Readers' Digest* may get their hands on it, and then, who knows . . .

Yes, Mrs DULCIE DOMUM of RUSBRIDGE, we wonder how many of your neighbours in CRANFORD GARDENS would be interested to know of your extra-marital activities two years ago. We guarantee that if you apply within fourteen days for your very own copy of *The Motorist's Guide to the 500 best British Lay-bys*, details of your affair with TOM THE PLUMBER will remain conveniently unknown in RUSBRIDGE and THE NATION AT LARGE.

fifty-two

'MUMMY! WHAT DOES *INTENSE* mean?'

'Well, it means sort of, er, fierce and strong and vivid.'

'What does *vivid* mean?'

'Er – oh, God – sort of fierce and strong and intense.'

Harriet runs off, apparently satisfied, leaving me limp with lexicographical effort. Admiration for Dr Johnson redoubled. Still, at least she didn't ask me what an orgasm was in front of Aunt Elspeth. Spouse dealt with this excruciating situation by declaring that he couldn't remember. Hm. There may be some truth in that.

The snowdrops, with courageous folly, are up and out. Would love to emulate them but, alas, fear I am more likely to achieve down and out. The Muse hath long been absent from my worm-eaten old desk. Shift my weight from one worm-eaten buttock to the other, and chew my pen. Recent silence from both Elaine-over-the-road and Tom suggests their *entente* may have become more *cordiale*. Did think, in one vain moment, that he might be desperate to grab my hands and say How could I possibly get interested in Elaine knowing that just across the road is the woman I love? I can *feel your vibes*, Dulcie, honest.

To be really honest, relief is the sensation uppermost in my mind. I have finished with vibes, nay, with all the paraphernalia of extra-curricular diversion. From now on my nose is firmly to the grindstone: dealing with my children's vocabularies and writing historical pulp fiction. Not a very intense destiny, to be sure: hardly vivid. But it is comfortable to know that one will not be required to present one's worm-eaten old buttocks to fervent young scrutiny in some fetid bedsit smelling of stale Marlboro and dirty socks.

Henry runs in and asks if he may have a Game Boy Compact Video System. 'It's only £89.99, Mum – you could give it me for an early birthday present.' Point out, with asperity, that his birthday is not until November and that, in my experience, Game Boys only lead to trouble.

'Anyway,' I warn, with awful seriousness, 'somebody told me that these computer thingies can cause fits.'

'What are fits?'

Harriet has sidled in, no doubt to keep a stern trades union eye on any concessions winkled out of me by Henry.

'Oh, Mum! That was only Mrs Twill! She's a *dinosaur*!'

'Henry! Don't be rude!'

'That's not rude, Mum. That's a fact!'

'Mrs Twill is *gruesome*!' Harriet always keen to join in any vilification available. 'Her utility room smells of *cats' piss*!'

'Where is Daddy?' Spouse is, in theory, in charge of them until two o'clock.

'He's mucking about in the garden.'

Odd. Spouse can be hardly be tempted into garden in mid-June with Brian Johnstone and deckchair. Refuse to speculate, however, about his activities; refuse to give a single further thought to delightful young plumber: grit teeth and leap into the so much more vivid and intense past.

Cleckthorpe, Gulpwell, Dronspit, Grindlow, Goytre . . . soon the train would arrive at Berpsover. Fanny's heart was soothed by the rhythm of the wheels on the rails, and her fancy was distracted from the mundane prospect of her home town and the rain-soaked cobbles of Blunkett Row, by the wild secret music of her imminent itinerary: Dover, Calais, and then, who knows? The crepuscular barges of Nougat-sur-Seine? The historic wharf at Frumpsvaart, scene of the assassination in 1599 of William the Garrulous? Why, thought Fanny, I might even hear the Lorelei sing.

Spouse appears abruptly in study, dishevelled and malodorous, and informs me that the ****ing drains are blocked – *again*. Is this A Sign?

fifty-three

ALAS! SPOUSE HAS MASTERFULLY summoned Dyno-rod before I have a chance to suggest that Tom's Buddhist/

Anarchist Plumbing Collective might be able to do the trick with a little gentle meditation. Have strange feeling of Unfinished Business in relation to Tom. But then, have feeling of Unfinished Business in relation to life in general, and feeling would only persist and intensify, I am sure, were I to live to 101.

Drains operative arrives in overalls and begins unpleasant activities resulting in horrid smell which permeates neighbourhood. Harriet runs in.

'Mummy, have you just farted?'

'Certainly not! It's the man outside unblocking our drains.'

'Brilliant!' Henry gazes admiringly out of window at Dynorod man. 'I wish I could do ones like that.'

Reluctantly concede that children may go out and watch – evidence, I suspect, of sloppy middle-class parenting. Spouse is out there, glaring down manhole cover in a way which suggests blockage is due entirely to me. He can, if necessary, prevent children falling into sludge, so I retire to bathroom and succour my olfactory senses with the remains of my Mitsouko. (Also worn, I believe, by Margaret Thatcher, so she can't be all bad.)

Sit on loo, then suddenly recall presence by manhole cover of Dyno-rod man and leap off again. Somehow feel that I am overlooked. Or underlooked, rather. Strange how when Dyno-rod man comes one is always faintly embarrassed that he should observe the evidence that one goes to the lavatory. Although Cosi Fan Tutti, after all. Except, of course, the Queen.

Phone rings. Leap to answer it in case it is Unfinished Business, but it is only Alice ringing up to gloat about her holiday in the West Indies. She rhapsodises about superiority of tropical climate, bus services, etc and eventually enquires how I am, how is the Bonkbuster coming along, has the heroine Fanny done the decent thing and joyfully acknowledged her lesbianism?

'Well, in a way,' I promise. 'She's escaped from the Hibernian Heathcliff and is following Gertrude across Europe.'

'Hibernian?' enquires Alice. 'I thought it was Scotland?'

'That's r – . . . Oh heck!'

'I've told you this before, Dulcie. Hi-ber-ni-a: Ireland. Cale-don-ia: Scotland. OK?'

'I know. I'm sorry. I can't seem to get it into my head. My brain's bunged up with all sorts of gunge. They've got a football team called Hibernian, you see. They do it on purpose to confuse me.' Alice forbids any further mention of soccer, that dreary spectacle of male bonding-and-roaring, and enquires belatedly how is Spouse.

'He's outside, supervising the Dyno-rod man.'

'The Dyno-rod man? Ah! The embodiment of the Pathetic Phallusy.'

Lavatory utters sudden alarming sound, as if it is going to be sick, giving me excuse to terminate call. But not before Alice has threatened to come and see us soon, and I have managed to sound delighted at the prospect. What a hero.

A grey smudge appeared on the horizon. That must be Calais, thought Fanny, clutching the ship's rail in relief. So what if she had been horribly seasick? It was appropriate, somehow: a symbol that she was leaving behind all that she had recently failed to digest: not merely her mother's haslet sandwiches, but the whole of the last year: the doomed passion she had shared on the slopes of Glen Close with Dougal MacPravity: her burgeoning friendship with Hector Macrae, nipped in the bud by that unfortunate landslide: indeed, the whole Hiber–Caledonian débâcle.

Too many colons in that passage. But then, too many colons on the planet as a whole. Fear *homo sapiens* may eventually drown in his own ordure. Although Chinese, apparently, recycle it all and manage to feed themselves on the resulting bamboo shoots and patchoi.

'I stink,' announces Spouse cheerfully. But fear it is only a physical description and not, as Alice would have wished, the dawning of an awareness of his paternalistic neo-colonial complacency.

fifty-four

INTERNATIONAL RUGBY SEASON IS in full swing. Spouse abandons all pretence of domestic duties, wraps himself in his dressing-gown, and sprawls on the sofa sipping Vermouth and wallowing in scrummage. He seems to be suffering from an attack of Les Fleurs du Mal Maninga.

I bet Baudelaire's mother never got any help with the washing-up. *Les sanglots longs / Des violons / Blessent mon cœur / D'un douleur / Monotone . . .* Or was that Verlaine? Very sixth form, anyway. But wait! My heroine Fanny, even now bracing herself for the wan embrace of Northern France, might meet some exotic poets in Paris.

With a plangent exhalation of steam, the locomotive Le Duc d'Asperges arrived at the Gare du Nord. Fanny grabbed her modest little carpet-bag and jostled her way through smoke, smuts and throng.

'Mademoiselle!' a cab-driver plucked at her sleeve, and asked her destination. [Indirect speech necessary as cannot remember French for 'Where to, luv?']

'L'Hôtel Rancide, Rue Beurre d'Anchois,' mumbled Fanny, ashamed of her halting accent. The cab moved off, and Fanny leaned back against the worn leather upholstery. Every bone in her body ached from the long journey. She would rest here for a few days before resuming her trans-European adventure. Gertrude had recommended the Hôtel Rancide, long ago in a French lesson at the Skinners Grammar School for Girls, Berpsover.

'If you ever find yourselves in Paris, girls, you can do no better than the Hôtel Rancide. It is on the Left Bank, in the Latin Quarter, the haunt of artists and poets. Guillaume Soutien-Gorge went into a decline there after the critics poured scorn on his third book of lyrics, Les Petits Navets. I always stay at the Rancide when I am in Paris.'

Fanny's heart missed a beat. Perchance Gertrude was here, now! She stared out eagerly into the gaily gaslit streets. [Check: was it gas in the 1900s? And was gas gay?]

A delicious smell wafted past. 'Oh qu'est-ce que c'est que cet arôme divine?' cried Fanny in ecstasy.

'C'est le Filet de Lièvre Poêlé à la Crème de Genièvre avec Fondue de Petits Pois et Laitue, Gratin de Topinambours, et pour le Dessert, Beignets d'Ananas au Coulis de Fruits de la Passion, Mademoiselle,' answered the cabbie dourly.

Convinced I should be making a better stab at Fanny's French episode had I to hand other books containing French words apart from Raymond Blanc's *Cooking for Friends* (self-serving, though wildly optimistic, birthday present from Spouse last year).

Feel hungry, and head for kitchen. As I pass sitting room, Spouse calls out from sofa in gently coaxing tone: 'I wouldn't say No to a cheese sandwich.'

'Perhaps you should have married one, then,' I retort with asperity, or perhaps with *asperges*. 'You say No to me often enough.'

All the same, I make him cheese sandwiches, knowing full well that, with ostentatious ineptitude, he will reduce the kitchen to rubble if left to do it himself. Am about to make cheese sandwich for myself when children arrive back from tea with Julian.

'We're starving, Mummy!' they cry, and devour all remaining bread and cheese before I can say *couteau*. Enquire why they are hungry since assume they were offered nourishment at Julian's.

'Ugh it was horrible foreign muck!' cries Henry. 'Left over from her dinner party last night. Can we have crisps and dip them in ketchup?'

Fear there is little chance of Henry growing up into a Raymond Blanc. Still, count blessings: not much chance of Baudelaire either.

'What are you two thinking of doing when you grow up?' I enquire sweetly.

'I'm going to be a vampire!' cries Harriet, grabbing the tomato ketchup and decorating her chin with it.

'I want to be a para, Mum,' admits Henry soberly. 'Only the trouble is, there may not be any more wars by the time I grow up.'

Assure son and heir that he will enjoy every opportunity to kill or be killed.

'Oh, why are men so *warish*?' roars Harriet. 'If I was Prime Minister I would *kill them all* except Daddy.'

fifty-five

FURTIVELY ATTEMPT TO THROW AWAY Christmas cards, but am arrested on verge of dustbin by indignant daughter.

'Stop, Mummy! Don't throw those angels away! I want them! For a collage of heaven!'

'All right – but throw away what you don't use, please.'

'You shouldn't put cardboard in the dustbin anyway. Miss Marsh says you should recycle it.'

Am getting rather sick of the infallible pronouncements of Miss Marsh. Still, infallibility a poor reward for enduring thirty-five seven-year-olds every day. Even beatification inadequate, in my view.

Attempt to create apple pie, sharing table with Harriet who gets herself into the right mood for creating heaven and earth by reading out all the old Christmas cards in a droning monotone.

'To wish you a Happy Christmas and a Preposterous New Year.'

Well, that's a safe bet, I should think.

Once 95 per cent of the table is covered with bits of cardboard, Harriet tires of heaven and earth and reverts to her preferred habit of raising hell.

'I know, Mummy! Let's make angels out of pastry and sell them to people we could put a sign up by the gate saying angels for sale oh please please please, Mummy!'

A wave of fatigue rises from the soles of my feet and demands that I sit down. Inform wave of fatigue that I am already seated. Try to summon up some encouraging enthusiasm for this evidence of my daughter's entrepreneurial spirit.

'Er, not now, Harriet. Next week, maybe.'

'You bastard, Mummy! I'm going up to my room and I'm never coming out never ever!'

She runs out, slamming the door. Several hundred severed limbs of angels swirl about in the draught, then float down to the kitchen floor, like something out of *Paradise Lost*, Book One.

Gaze wanly at debris. Of course she should be made to clear up her mess, but know full well it would require half an hour of arguing, so clear it up myself in thirty seconds. *I am in parental inadequacy stepped in so far . . . Returning were as tedious as go o'er*. Macbeth. Only in his case, it was not parental inadequacy but murder. Well, same thing, really.

Complete pie, decorate with wan and soggy sprig of pastry leaves, and think how much more glorious pie would have been in hands of Benvenuto Cellini. Or even anybody else at all. Place pie in oven, which is beginning to stink and smoke like some dismal charcoal-burner's device in pre-Revolutionary Russia. From Gorky's *My Childhood*, perhaps.

Count blessing: Spouse and Henry at Rugby match. Switch on Radio Four for comfort fix, but it is the News: child murder again. Switch off again and snivel for a few minutes into kitchen paper. Seem to have wept a lot recently, but no happy tears except when watching dog-and-loo-paper ad. Above the indignant hissing and growling of the oven can hear Harriet also weeping bitterly upstairs.

Spouse, were he here, would utter stern injunction to let her stew in her own juice. This is as near as he ever gets to helping with the cooking. Heave sigh, go upstairs and knock on her door.

'Go away for ever!'

Know that this means Please Come In Immediately, so enter and hug, as instructed by Princess of Wales. Apologies exchanged, etc. Harriet recovers her imperious energy.

'I know, Mummy! Let's have pancakes like last week!'

'Well, just a minute – I must have a pee first.'

As I am pulling up my knickers afterwards, however, somehow an earring falls down lavatory. Have to grope about horridly in own pee to rescue it, and in doing so, carelessly submerge watch.

Rinse hands, and watch, and earring, whilst Harriet nags and knocks without, 'What are you *doing*, Mummy?' Reach up and open medicine cabinet for headache pill, and whole glass bottleful (500) falls out heavily on to nose with loud crack. Haven't cried so much since five minutes ago.

Am trying unsuccessfully to think of an appropriate quotation, when doorbell rings. It is Alice, two weeks early and accompanied by beautiful freckly woman who is Not Saskia. Just hope that, when it comes to pancakes, she is an ace tosser.

fifty-six

ALICE'S FRIEND IS THE splendid speckly Elly. 'Is it short for Elephant, Mummy?' whispers Harriet. One does not enquire after Saskia. One fears she may have gone the way of Lymeswold and Izal. To be honest, I prefer Elly. Saskia slopped about all morning, spreading stale crusts and fag-ash over the kitchen table, but Elly always gets to the sink first and scrubs everything till it shines. She also genuinely likes children, and soon has them making Welsh cakes (ingredients from a large box of groceries she has brought). Alice is madly in love, and suspect that I may soon join her.

Spouse goes down with massive cold, and retires to camp bed in his study. Lament that bed is the only camp thing about Spouse. Harriet joins me in matrimonial bed, vacating her bed for Alice and Elly. We did not have time to hide the Sindy dolls but, under Elly's influence, Alice has softened towards them. She insists they are female impersonators and calls them Harold, Joe, Pete and Fred.

Alice shows polite and Elly genuine interest in the progress of my Bonkbuster. Promise to show them a bit of it. Elly volunteers to take children to park whilst I finish off latest chapter in way which I hope will be acceptable to our guests.

So this was Paris! Fanny stood on the tiny balcony of her room and looked out across the roofs and spires. Instead of the stink of slag-heaps, there was the delicious scent of roasting chestnuts. Instead of the gloomy outline of the Guscott and Pikelet Steel Truss Company, the distant buttresses of Notre Dame leapt gracefully upwards in the twilight. And immediately below, in the service courtyard of the Hôtel Rancide, someone was peeling not the humble potato but that enigmatic, that exotic tuber, the Jerusalem artichoke.

Oh, if only Gertrude was here to share this magic moment! Fanny's heart pounded at the memory of her friend's wise green eyes and strong, fervent spirit. The youth peeling the artichokes somehow sensed her presence, looked upward, and uttered a foolish tweeting sound. 'Delicieuse petite anglaise!' he whispered – or something of the sort. Fanny glared, darted back indoors, and slammed the shutters. Trust a mere man to spoil her moment of crepuscular calm.

Aware that Lucien Penible, poet and necromancer, is lounging downstairs in the hotel bar, but do not think it advisable to impose him on Fanny until Alice and Elly have gone.

Emerge for tea and find Alice deep in the Newnham College Roll Letter. Elly is still out at the park.

'Listen to this, Dulcie!' she exclaims. 'Someone's been publishing papers on "Formation and regeneration of rhombomere boundaries in the developing chick hindbrain". Not to mention "Knowledge of arm position under varied gravitoinertial force in parabolic flight".'

Wonder if perhaps my own education was wasted, and observe that there ain't half been some clever bastards.

'Science . . .' sighs Alice. 'A whole frigging galaxy of knowledge, in which we will never so much as dip a timid toe.'

Heroically forbear to point out the mixed metaphor, and, since Elly is absent, enquire what happened to Saskia.

'Well, you know how it is, Dulcie – once I'd met Elly, everything else just fell to bits.'

Suppress qualm of jealousy at the way Alice's life conveniently disintegrates and re-forms itself around new delights, like a wave o'the sea. Own life more akin to badly cracked plate, bolted and glued together in crude way which would appal experts on *The Antiques Roadshow*. Make a few polite references to Saskia's sterling but now apparently irrelevant qualities, and then cut my losses and start to praise Elly.

Immediately Alice's eyes brim with the foolish effulgence of love, but, thank God, children suddenly burst in. Loud uproar of Guess Who We Met in the Park, and Elly cries, with conjuring air as practised by Rosalind at end of *As You Like It*: 'Here's an old friend of yours, Dulcie! Henry and Harriet asked him back for tea, so I bought a couple of packets of crumpets. It's Tom!' Though Elly has only just met Tom, there is something so monstrously proprietorial about the way she introduces me to my own ex-lover, that I yearn, briefly, for her sudden death.

fifty-seven

'DO YOU FANCY A bit of crumpet, Tom?' Thus does the scintillating Elly tempt my ex-lover with her steaming delicacies. We all laugh obediently, then Harriet whispers, 'Mummy what are we laughing at?'

Tom watches Elly's toastings and butterings with fascinated smile, as though she were performing magic rites on sacred Tibetan gongs. Children are already completely in her power, Harriet re-created as Elly's Little Jellybaby and Henry as Doctor Mad.

'And how about you, Dulcie?' Elly fixes me with her gorgeous green eyes and offers me a crumpet glistening with butter. 'Marmite or my home-made goosegog jam?'

Decide I might as well capitulate to her goosegogs. It's too late to worry about being too fat. Besides, Tom has not looked me in the eye once since he came in, let alone looked me in the hip.

'Have you got a gooseberry bush in Hackney, then?' I enquire.

'Oh no dear, I get 'em orf me old ma in the country. Dorset.'

'Dorset!' cries Tom with foolish ecstasy. Tempted to inform him that Dorset is only a county, but manage to zip lip. 'Oh, that's my absolute favourite place. Ghosts and stuff, right? Atmosphere – terrific!' Convinced he would have said the same had her old ma lived in Dagenham.

'More crumpets, kiddos? What would you like on yours this time, Doctor Mad? Peanut butter and woodlice poo?'

Oh, how jolly vivacious she is, and what a creative imagination. Oh, how we all laugh. Can't help noticing, though, that Alice is beginning to gnaw her fingers – always a sign of emotional, and occasionally international, tension. Wonder if she is wondering, as I am, whether Elly is reliably lesbian.

'So what do you do, Tom, when not idling around on park benches and picking your nose?'

'Tom's a plumber!' yells Henry. 'But I'm going to be a para!'

'A plumber!' Elly literally falls to her knees before him. 'Oh, thank you, God! Please, please, Mr Plumber, come to Hackney and plumb in my new central heating system. It's been in pieces on the floor for weeks. Since Aziz let me down.'

Well, how could he refuse? Alice and I try, heroically, to looked pleased at the sight of our friends getting on so well.

'Actually, I'm not doing plumbing full-time now,' admits Tom with a fey wriggle. 'I'm, like, getting into healing.'

I do not like *like*. Recall that at crucial moments Tom was always able to rile me with some infelicity of grammar. Thank you God, I see you have not forgotten me, either.

'A healer! How perfect! As you can see, I am unravelling rather fast in all directions!' Elly trills with the conscious pleasure of one who has not, so far, even snagged herself slightly on one of the splinters of Time.

The door opens and Spouse appears, wrapped in dressing-gown and looking not unlike Sherlock Holmes after a binge. Feel inexplicable wave of affection for him, but before I can hoist myself up out of chair Elly has waltzed past me and is drawing him into her charmed circle and offering him crumpets, tea, her warmed seat, etc. Spouse stiffly resists, but Elly says she will cuddle up with her Little Jellybaby and would he like Marmite or gooseberry jam on it?

'I have always rather baulked at crumpets,' says Spouse sternly. 'They look to me, somehow, like an eighteenth-century contraceptive.' Merry peals of laughter at this sally. Harriet, on Elly's knee, asks in vain What is a Contraceptive. Then even Spouse – *Et tu*, you Brute – succumbs to her blandishments and says perhaps he will make an exception just this once, as he has always liked a bit of gooseberry jam on his contraceptives.

'So: how's life treating the Buddhist/Anarchist artisan, these days?' enquires Spouse with a charming smile the like of which he never bestowed on Tom back in the bad old days when I was in charge round here. Feel the moment has come to slip away to my dear old faithful lavatory. My last, truest friend, offering silence and repose.

As I sit down, however, the seat skids violently to the right, depositing me on the bathroom floor. Oh God. I am usurped as mother, mistress, wife: now apparently even the lav prefers her. Lie on the floor for some minutes before consoling myself that nobody is going to notice even if I have, by some rough magic, been turned into a gooseberry fool.

fifty-eight

'SO: WHEN CAN YOU come and sort out my central heating, Tom?' Elly settles down to a bit of serious plumber-stealing.

'It seems a bit pointless to have it sorted out at this time of year,' carps Alice, evidently panicking at the thought of Tom tinkering dexterously with Elly's thermostats. 'I mean, it's almost summer.'

'What crap you talk, Ally,' sneers Elly. 'You know how cold-blooded I am. It snowed in May once when I lived in Islip. So' – she turns her great green magnetising globes on Tom, and revs them up to maximum appeal – 'how soon can you make it, Maestro?'

'Well, the next month is going to be a bit hectic,' confesses Tom with a demure smile at his knees. 'You see, I'm getting married on the 3rd of April.'

'Getting married?' I shriek. 'Congraaaaaaaaaghtulations!'

'Marriage?' ponders Alice. 'How quaint. I didn't think young people did that sort of thing nowadays.'

'Of course they do, Ally!' retorts Elly scathingly. 'Young people believe in romance and fidelity and stuff. How wonderful, Tom! Who is she?'

'She's called Sabrina.' For the first time since he entered the room, Tom looks at me: a look at once timid and defiant. But I am ready for him: in the ten seconds available since his announcement, I have managed to veil my secret agony in a deranged leer.

'Sabrina!' I cry in synthetic ecstasy. 'The goddess of the River Severn!'

'In my day,' observes Spouse crisply, 'Sabrina was a minor actress with massive tits.'

Children instantly dissolve into raucous yells of laughter.

'What does she do, Tom?' asks Elly, evidently ready to be delighted, whatever it is.

'She's a stone mason,' replies Tom, with satisfaction.

'A stone mason! But how *marvellous*!'

Feel that, compared to Sabrina the stone mason, I am a very dull dog indeed.

Harriet comes up to me shyly and whispers, 'Mummy, will you please ask Tom if I can be his bridesmaid?'

'And . . .' Tom confides proudly, as if revealing the acme of Sabrina's accomplishments, 'she's a Taurus with the moon in Venus!' For some reason this makes me feel a bit better.

A few days later, Elly and Ally depart, and I decide to clear out my bra drawer. My bras are all useless now. One is too large, provoking feelings of inadequacy. One is too small across the back, one too low-cut, leading to asymmetrical escapes; another's hooks are hanging by a thread. Bras resemble matrimony, really: designed to yoke together in comfort, but in the event, always disappointing.

Phone rings: it is Aunt Elspeth. She is going to send me £10 to buy a bird-table for Harriet's birthday.

'It's such a wonderful sight, dear!' she trills. 'I've got the cheekiest little tits up here.' Like idea of birds. Need a hobby to take my mind off gorgeous Sabrina and her blasted chisels.

Aunt Elspeth's £10 does not go very far towards a bird-table, so am obliged to augment the fund. Console myself by sending away for Ivory Stretch Lace Bra with Softly Gathered Effect, by mail order.

Birds congregate obligingly on bird-table. Call Harriet, who says, 'I'll come in a minute, Mummy! After *Batman*!' Ring Aunt Elspeth who congratulates me.

'My tits respond very well to fat balls, dear.'

Rush out and buy four huge fat balls at £1.25 each as recommended by Danish Ornithological Society, though fail to read instructions till later and therefore neglect to squeeze balls before hanging.

Glued to window for hours: domestic tasks accumulate in vain. Devour Spouse's old bird book, and become ludicrously ambitious. Four different sorts of tit not enough: long for our bird-table to be visited by Isabelline Shrike, Slate-Coloured Junco, Blue-Cheeked Bee-Eater, or Noddy.

Bra delivered. Put it on: terrible itching springs up between shoulder-blades, but cannot be bothered to send it back. Tempted to hang all bras up in old apple tree for birds to nest in, but afraid Bernard Twill next door might find it all too distracting.

fifty-nine

RUSH ACROSS ROAD AT first opportunity to divulge to Elaine the awful news that Tom is to marry a stone mason called Sabrina.

'I know: isn't it wonderful!' she cries. 'What are you going to wear?'

My face falls with a resounding crash on to the chic Mexican tiles of Elaine's kitchen.

'Oh, Dulcie! Don't say he hasn't asked you?'

Affirm that this is indeed the case, but assure her vigorously that Tom's wedding is not one I would be particularly anxious to attend.

'Of course!' soothes Elaine. 'You're his, er, sort of Camilla Parker-Bowles, aren't you?'

This evidently meant to cheer me up, though I always sympathise more with Andrew Parker-Bowles. If I was him, I'd let 'em have it with both barrels.

'But anyway,' continues Elaine, 'he's no more than getting even with you, really, is he? I mean you've been married all along.'

Realise this is true, but somehow it seems like a *non sequitur*.

Enquire, as casually as possible, if Elaine has any further information about Sabrina.

'Yes, I've met her actually. It was a bit of a whirlwind thing, I gather.'

It must have been: Tom was in a desultory way pretending to date Elaine herself in the fairly recent past. Wonder that she does not feel miffed thereat.

'Oh no, Dulcie!' she cries. 'He's not my type at all – in fact I think your dear Spouse is far far sexier, to be honest.'

Ignoring this lamentable lapse of taste, I express the spurious hope that Sabrina is extraordinarily beautiful.

'Oh no!' cries Elaine warmly. 'Quite short and to tell you the truth, a bit stout. Short black curly hair, no neck, big biceps but you'd expect that in a stone mason wouldn't you? Wears dungarees, smokes roll-ups and must be at least thirty-five because her sons' voices have broken.'

Although seated, cannot help staggering at this news.

'Not a patch on you for beauty, Dulcie,' concludes Elaine, with delectable dishonesty. Resolve to nominate her for a peerage immediately.

Elaine concludes her description of Sabrina with the fascinating detail that she wears a jewel in the side of her nose.

Have always wondered how people manage to do that, and what happens when they blow it.

On way back home, pause to stroke the Twills' splendid tomcat Bertie, sunning himself on the wall. Envy his lifestyle, uncomplicated by matrimony – only surpassed in its elegant simplicity by that of hermaphroditic earthworm. Inform myself sternly that I am glad that Tom is to marry not a vapid bimbo but a woman of maturity and character, and re-enter house.

Spouse is reading sports page. Scrutinise him thoroughly: Spouse raises enquiring eyebrow: report that Elaine said he was sexy.

'I was once told,' he informs me modestly, 'that I had the best balls in Balliol.' Refrain from asking By Whom and hope he is disappointed.

Right, well, terrific! This Sabrina business is the best thing that could possibly happen. My life energy will be forced to spring off in exciting new directions, like a recently pruned rose. Oh heck! Have not yet pruned roses. Cannot find secateurs, so go out into garden armed with old pair of nail scissors.

Return defeated and bleeding five minutes later to find Spouse watching Italian football. Wonder if this could be exciting new direction for my life energies. TV reveals archetypal Latin lover, presumably managerial, gesturing despairingly from sidelines.

'Who's that?'

'Dinner's off.'

Further enquiries elucidate: manager in question is apparently called Dino Zoff. Instantly abandon plans for torrid affair with him. His name would always remind me of my domestic inadequacies.

Go to kitchen, sigh deeply, and start to peel potatoes. Oh well. There's always the bird-table. Gaze out, but horror! Behold the Twills' cat with a greenfinch in his mouth. *Et tu*, Bertie? Scream, run outdoors, and kick furry arse with a vehemence which surprises even myself. He's done it: the worst cruelty possible – he's marrying a *younger* older woman, dammit.

sixty

So: Tom is married. He sent me a card which arrived the day before which read: *I'm sure you don't want to come to the wedding which will be full of boring relatives and stuff but I'm dying for you to meet Sabrina and will ring you when we get back from our 'honeymoon'(!)*

Recall wise words of my English Teacher when I had used inverted commas to distance myself from a word which might be interpreted as 'slightly naff'. She wrote: *If you have to apologise for it, don't use it.* So much for 'honeymoon', let alone (!). Wonder where they have gone, and hope he does not have the lack of tact to send me a postcard. *Wish you were here . . .* Wherever they are, must be constantly vigilant lest I start to think: *Wish I was there . . .*

Perhaps I should have sent him a pair of celebratory cufflinks with our initials linked together: D and T. The DTs. Perhaps that is my destiny. Admit to having knocked back a couple of bottles of Sauvignon entirely unassisted during the past week. Must pull myself together and get on with Bonkbuster. Fanny has been waiting to go down to dinner in the Hôtel Rancide for at least a month. The poor girl must be ravenous.

But first, a letter from Alice, who has taken Elly to Salamanca. It would have been tactless to go for Santiago de Compostela, I suppose: scene of her scene with Saskia. Alice reports that the Spaniards call Prince Charles 'Lord Tampax' and that during a recent carnival procession the students all dressed up as tampons, with Prince Charles masks on their heads.

Utter brief but heartfelt prayer of thanks that I am not a member of the royal family nor one of its confidants.

'Mummee! Can we have oven chips and veggy fingers? Perleeze!'

Switch on oven to maximum. Need to nourish children comes, for once, as a relief from intolerable oscillation between anguish and anomie. Feel sudden urge to commit same to paper so tell children they are to wash up and I will be back in fifteen minutes to dish up. Rush to study and seize pen.

Fanny stepped self-consciously down into the mahogany and eau-de-nil lobby of the Hôtel Rancide. She was aware that her grey worsted dress was shabby and still smut-strewn from the journey. The receptionist beckoned her with a sour air. Oh heavens! Would he complain about her ensemble? But no. He handed her a letter with a thin and sallow smile.

'Pour vous, Mademoiselle.'

Fanny recognised the neat, small hand of Hector Macrae, her former headmaster at Auchtereekie. So, he was recovered enough to communicate! Fanny tore the letter open and devoured its contents.

> *Dear Fanny, I hope this finds you in health: mine improves so much that I am able to ramble again over the slopes of Glen Close. I have some news which will surprise, but I hope will please you. My sister Mairi married the pastor Dougal MacPravity on Wednesday last. He is a changed man since you left: converses civilly with everyone, and is full of tender solicitude towards my sister. Though the speed with which they came to an understanding may surprise some, I am confident of her happiness. And my dear Fanny, freed of the necessity of being my sister's keeper, I must now ask you to look favourably upon a suit which I have long longed to press upon you. Though you are far away, there is not an hour of the day when I do not think of you with the most ardent sensations. I will not be content till you are blowing my eggs and helping me to press my Corn-Cockle, Hare's-Foot and Frog-Bit. Will you be my wife?'*

Uttering a weak cry not unlike that of a fainting and famished fledgling curlew, Fanny fell insensible upon the hotel carpet. Lucien Penible, who had been sipping absinthe in a corner, leapt to his feet and whipped out his smelling salts –

'Mummee! The sink's bunged up!' How accurately does the plumbing mock my emotional state. Hasten to kitchen, where am greeted not just by blocked sink but also by horrible smell suggestive of industrial accident in USSR. Something wrong with oven: peer inside and see previously unsuspected breadknife, handle of which has melted all over oven chips on shelf below. Is this a symbol? Switch off oven, open windows, order children out of area, fling open cupboard under sink, and with massive strength born of despair, unscrew trap and cover self, floor and all Mrs Body's neatly-folded dusters with great stinking gouts of black gunge.

sixty-one

The prone Fanny's eyelids flickered. Voices whirled and rang in her fevered brain. 'Mademoiselle! . . . Taisez-vous . . . Ah, mon Dieu!' A corner of ceiling and wall appeared in her vision. Fanny recognised it as an architectural detail of the lobby of the Hôtel Rancide, Paris. To her horror she realised she had fainted. She only hoped she had done it in French.

'Mademoiselle . . .' A face appeared, that of a young man with a long pale face. Chestnut curls clustered on his collar; his lips were a perfect Cupid's bow, and beyond the overpowering reek of smelling-salts which he proffered, Fanny's alert nostrils registered a faint whiff of Hergé's Eau de Snowy.

'Eet ees all wight, Mademoiselle,' lisped the Cupid's bow. Fanny clutched convulsively at his helpful hand.

'I'm so sorry – I must have fainted.'

'Finque nuzzingue orpheet,' he soothed, dismissing the intrusive crowd of spectators which had gathered, and helping her to a shabby chair in the corner of the bar.

'Une tasse de thé pour Mademoiselle!' he called, and Fanny managed a wan smile between the qualms of vertigo which still surged in her brain.

'You 'ave receive ze barde neuws?' he enquired, indicating the letter which she still held, crumpled, to her bosom. Fanny sighed.

'Just that – someone I rather cared for has married the sister of – of someone else I rather cared for,' she whispered.

'Ah, you 'ave ze too tendre 'art, comme moi,' nodded her rescuer. 'I also 'ad a friend I razza cared for. 'Is name was Philippe Larquin . . . he was, how we say, joli laid, but hélàs! Not by me.'

Fanny could not quite interpret his melancholy anecdote, but was cheered, soon after, by the arrival of a glass of tea and two dry almond biscuits.

How strangely incompetent the French were, though, in the matter of biscuits and cakes! Fanny endured a pang of longing for her mother's glistening lardy collops . . .

Phone rings. It has been so, all afternoon, ever since I sat down to Bonkbuster. First it was someone enquiring for the crematorium (a wrong number, but nevertheless, like single magpies, strangely lowering, somehow). Then a call from a charity asking me to give them money by covenant; then another call from the same charity expressing the hope that I was not in any way inconvenienced by the first call . . . Then a call from a colleague of Spouse's to say Forget it he doesn't need it, then a call from Mrs Body to say she doesn't think she'll be able to make it tomorrow as she feels a bit queer.

Ring, ring, ring, ring – like a frantic toddler suffering from separation anxiety, unable to amuse itself quietly for even five minutes. Suddenly see British Telecom as a vast nervous system, messages flashing up and down the national body politic, from Buddy can you spare a dime to I wish I was a tampax. Perhaps if I was a French choreographer I would find inspiration in it: *Prélude à l'après midi d'un phone.*

What is it this time? Seize receiver and identify myself with ferocious bark.

'Hi, Dulcie, this is Tom! We just got back from San Gimignano, and guess what! It rained!'

Express incredulity and outrage.

'Anyway, we'd like to come and see you. Sabrina's, like, dying to meet you and, well, nothing's going down here right now, so why not right now?'

Suppress the memory of when Tom used to ring up and say *why not right now* because he couldn't wait to see me. Now he can't wait to introduce his wife to me. However, insist that now couldn't be better, i.e. obediently and gracefully lay down head on block.

Once phone replaced, panic. Am dirty, smelly, unkempt, and hands look 2000 years old. Rush to bathroom and apply hand–cream Not Tested on Animals. What animals could one test hand–cream on? Moles, I suppose.

Enter Harriet. 'Mummy! How *exactly* does the man get the baby–seeds inside the lady?'

Hastily outline aforementioned process.

'Ugh!' cries Harriet. 'How disgusting! Still, if you don't want to have babies you don't have to do it, do you?'

sixty-two

LIFE IS FULL OF awkwardnesses, but being introduced to one's ex-lover's shiny new wife must take the cake. This would explain perhaps why the cake-tin is empty – another embarrassment. Manage to prise fossilised dollops of food off the kitchen table, scoop all dirty dishes into a carrier-bag and place in broom cupboard, and fling long-dead daffodils into long-ignored compost bucket under sink.

Why does ex-daffodil-water smell so vile? Rather than pollute whole kitchen with the pong, carry stinking vase upstairs and secrete within wardrobe. Rush to bathroom to examine face, and trip over that charmless object, still-full but stone-cold hot water bottle, lying in middle of floor. Unscrew with great difficulty because of recently moisturised hands, but am glad to notice *en glissant* that hands look 1000 years younger – i.e. only 999 years old.

Drape hot water bottle across edge of washbasin so it can empty itself therein. Stare into mirror. Horror! Large spot rising angrily on chin, like one of Fungus the Bogeyman's boils. Grab cosmetic Coverstick with which to camouflage it. Undue haste causes stick to fly from its holster and fall beneath washbasin. Bend to retrieve it and knock hot water bottle off its delicate axis. Hot water bottle performs somersault, drenching hair, glasses and shoulders with cold water smelling faintly like Lapsang Souchong.

Coverstick now adorned with bits of fluff and grit, but roll it on none the less, hoping for camouflage. Alas, presence of spot is now signposted by shrieking smudge of peach goo and small goatee beard of fluff and grit. Wipe it all off, at which spot starts to flash painfully like Belisha beacon. Front doorbell rings. Oh hell.

Oh well. At least hands only look 999 years old. Descend, open door, and manage at last minute to cram myself into gracious welcoming smile, although much too tight, and seams rip audibly at the sight of Tom's arm round Sabrina's shoulders. An unnecessary error of taste, I feel.

Note that Sabrina has also had the lack of tact to discard what one hoped was her habitual boilersuit and is arrayed in black mini and tights, ensemble which somehow does not look too young on her, but which, were I to attempt, would raise the spectre of mammoth dressed as lamb.

Ushering them into the kitchen, I cannot help noticing that Sabrina's bum sticks out in the satisfactory pneumatic style perfected by the Bushwomen of the Kalahari. Mine more reminiscent of Barbara Bush than Bushwoman.

Realise that in describing Sabrina as 'stocky', Elaine was nursing my wounded ego. She is, in fact, stocky in the right places and, though allegedly at least thirty-five, has the glowing rounded cheeks and black curls of a Caravaggio boy. How has she managed this? Old Holborn, perhaps, for she is working on her first roll-up within seconds of sitting down.

Manage to make cup of tea whilst casually covering spot most of the time with my strikingly rejuvenated left hand, and keeping my grandmotherly bum turned away from guests.

Tom gasses away about Tuscany, but cannot hear a word. I am waiting for Sabrina to speak. So far he has spoken for her, e.g. 'Sabrina's been dying to meet you', and 'Is it OK if Sabrina smokes?' Am curiously keen to hear her voice delivering an extended sentence. The eyes may be the windows of the soul but the tongue sure tells more tales than it knows. Eventually resort to the Direct Question.

'What are you chipping away at at the moment?' (Apart from my self-esteem, of course.)

Sabrina blows a funnel of smoke in my direction and looks at me witheringly for several seconds. Then: 'About half a ton of Portland stone.'

Am silenced, though feel there is a certain macho brutality about her reply.

'Tom tells me you write bodice rippers. You don't, do you? *Really?*'

The deep scorn and incredulity behind this utterance confirms that Sabrina speaks from a position of High Moral Seriousness. This relegates me to position of Low Immoral Frivolity: my favourite. Relieved, by Sabrina's hostility, of the effort of trying to like her, I spend rest of their visit gleefully boring them with tedious details of recent rips.

Have never waved Tom out with greater pleasure, and when Spouse arrives home, unnerve him with welcoming kiss. Two days later, however, remember that daffodil-water still in wardrobe, and discover it has emptied itself into my best red suede shoes.

sixty-three

AM DEPRESSED ABOUT *The Archers*. The lovely Caroline throwing herself away on that neurasthenic vicar – or is he a vet? And how could anybody possibly be a convincing vet half the time and a vicar the other? Afterbirths before lunch, afterlife after?

And another thing. Can't help being irritated by the TV adverts for sanitary protection, despite knowing that my attitude to The Vagina ought to be a venal veneration for the Goddess, the life-source, etc, unlike Lear's view of women, more generally widespread I suspect:

But to the girdle do the Gods inherit,
Beneath is all the fiends':
There's hell, there's darkness, there's the sulphurous pit,
Burning, scalding, stench, consumption; fie, fie, fie! pah, pah!

Well, thank God for Sloggi Maxis, I suppose.

What? Lit Crit before breakfast? Well, why not? My ex-lover is safely married to a woman of stone. One does like to find good homes for them. Now, after twenty years of oblivion, perchance Lit Crit may beckon again. But then again, perchance not. Reach for the Coco Pops. First one must feed the Inner Critic.

Count blessings. At least all traces of Easter eggs gone, leaving not a wrack behind save Aunt Elspeth's gift vouchers. ('I don't approve of too much chocolate for the bairns, dearr.')

Speaking of which, Harriet runs in, sees vouchers and is seized by greed.

'Mummee! Can I spend my git voucher?'

'Sensible of her to get them git vouchers,' observes Spouse behind the *Observer*. 'There is such a variety of gits available these days.'

Once upon a time one could have said, Sorry darling but the shops are shut: it's Sunday. But not any more. Not sure which is worse: children being possessed by Mammon or Sega. Suspect mass-hypnotism of the world's young by electronic games is a masterly plan for eventual bloodless coup by clever things from neighbouring galaxy,

'Henry! There are little green men training their ray-guns on me! Help!'

'Just a *minute*, Mum! I'm in the middle of a *game*!'

Rifle through yesterday's junk mail, and find Invitation to a Private View, with picture of Mr and Mrs Robert Andrews by Thomas Gainsborough, apparently A Study in Refinement. I always thought they looked a pretty poisonous pair of little shits, or perhaps gits, presiding tight-lipped over their acres. Give me Hogarth's servants any day for humanity, even if they did stink a bit.

Have to admit, however, that brochure's next offering: Henri Rousseau's *Tropical Storm with Tiger* does suggest The Importance of Stealth, and Berthe Morisot's tender mother-and-baby study *The Cradle* might well resonate with That Vital Element of Tranquillity.

Then discover whole caboodle is an advertising blurb for the New Safrane by Renault: A Study in Refinement, providing The Vital Element of Tranquillity, etc. 'In short, the Safrane by Renault is the intelligent alternative for those who are able to *resist the obvious* executive car.' Fie, fie, fie! Pah, pah! I bet Mr and Mrs Snooty Robert Andrews would have snapped one up. Too glossy for bum-fodder, so throw in recycling box.

Take children to Garden Centre where everything else is for sale as well, except what Henry wants: video games. Harriet selects Jojoba Oil bubble bath in beguiling pack adorned with nostalgic deco artwork of two nymph-like children taking a bath in a huge shell floating on the waves. Fetching, reminiscent of Birth of Venus, etc.

Upon closer inspection, discover that it says Jojoba Oil (0.1%). What does this mean? That it is only a thousandth part Jojoba Oil? If so, isn't that like calling the Ministry of Education the Ministry of Education? What's really in this bath stuff, then? Sodium Laureth Sulfate, Lauramide Dea,

Water Butylparaben . . . Ethylparaben . . . I feel a pong coming on . . . *Oh Lauramidea! Ethyl is such a paragon, a real buty, she really bowls me over: Laureth is a breath of fresh sulfate but where the hell is the Jojoba?*

sixty-four

As Fanny sipped her thé and nibbled the strange dry French almond biscuits (What were they called? Madeleines?) Lucien Penible ransacked his pockets and produced a dog-eared notebook.

'*Eef you are fillingue bettaire, Mademoiselle, pair apse I may h'asque your h'advice?*'

'*Oh, certainement!*'

'*I h'am as I 'ave h'indiquated a poète – eef you permet, I h'am maquingue a translation of my* Petites Noisettes *into ze* Eengleesh . . .'

He thrust the book into her hand. Fanny opened it and found many lyrics scribbled in violet ink. She bent her luminous orbs upon page one.

> *O soldier O poet*
> *Of the body white*
> *Lead me through your sighs*
> *To the vibrating kidneys*
> *Of your midnight.*

'*Why, it is exquisite!*' *murmured Fanny.* '*But might I suggest "trembling loins" in line 4? "Vibrating kidneys" is somewhat medical, I find.*'

'*Ah, Mademoiselle! You 'ave ze –* 'ow you say? Sensibilité! *Are you pair apse a student of ze poesie?*'

'*Oh wee!*' *ejaculated Fanny with enthusiasm – and prepared to embark on a series of admiring remarks about Coleridge's* Frost at Midnight *(Gêlée a Minuit, surely – or should that be Glace? Or was one of them a pudding? – How treacherous was the Gallic tongue!) Before she could commence, however, a confident footstep broke into their entente and a hearty English voice rang out.*

'*Lucien! Sorry I'm late, old chap – I was detained in a pissoir behind La Madeleine.*'

Fanny look up, intrigued by this reference to biscuits, and beheld a tall slim Englishman with piercing blue eyes. Why, thought Fanny, his golden hair spirals away from his temples like the wings on the helmet of the god Mercury! His blue stare washed over her, and, confused, she dropped her gaze to the knees of his tweed knickerbockers – like Plus Fours only somewhat shorter. Petits Fours, perhaps.

'Ah, a fellow-countrywoman, I ween. Allow me to introduce myself. Edgar Percy Houseboy of Much Lovelock in Shropshire. Percy to my devotees – of which there are all too few, alas!'

'Fanny Hoddle,' murmured Fanny awkwardly. 'Of Berpsover. You are a poet too, Mr Houseboy?'

'Oh, a scribbler!' Percy Houseboy flung himself down beside Lucien Penible, seized the Frenchman's hand, and much to Fanny's astonishment, kissed it. How extravagant folks' manners seemed to be in Shropshire! 'Compared to dear Lucien's majestic Noisettes*, my stuff is mere doggerel!' Lucien's cupid's bow lips dismissed this with a self-depreciating pout. Percy pulled a sheaf of papers from his pocket and tossed them into Fanny's lap. She read at random.*

> *The shepherd's pectorals as he leans, a-shearing*
> *Athwart the lucky sheep*
> *With every glistening drip recall*
> *How in an Olympian clearing*
> *Athenian athletes wrestled all*
> *Ungirt – but I have promises to keep*
> *And cannot stay here, leering.*

'Oh, how beautiful!' cried Fanny. 'One can almost smell the sweat, can one not?'

'What eez your poison, Squire?' enquired Lucien of the windswept Englishman. Percy clapped a hearty hand on the worn velvet of Lucien's slender knee, cried, 'Mine's a ploughman!' and winked at Fanny. Not knowing what response was proper, Fanny winked back, though her brain was whirling. What could it all mean?

'Mummee!' Harriet runs in with the post: one letter. 'Daddy says there is no such thing as heaven. What if he's right! Oh hell!' She bursts into tears. Assure her that Daddy is always wrong, but if there's no heaven we can all turn into wild flowers instead. Although suspect the best one can hope for these days is a gladiolus. Peruse letter, from agent Penelope. 'Don't want to nag, but trust Fanny is bonking her way relentlessly across Europe.'

sixty-five

ROADWORKS IN RUSBRIDGE: IN order to complete school run am obliged to take tedious detour down narrow winding lane. Suddenly, scruffy lorry hurtles round corner towards us. Close eyes and lurch sideways on to verge enabling him to roar past us.

Shaking, I shout, *The Bastard! The Bastard!* and explain to children that we have just avoided death by a millimetre.

'Did we nearly die, Mummy?' shrieks Harriet. 'The bastard!'

'I'll kill him!' cries Henry. 'The bastard! The bastard! The bastard!'

'Er – that's enough bastards, Henry.'

'But you –!'

'I know, I know, but – you know.'

Recognising the truck as part of the outfit doing the roadworks, I vow that on the way back I shall stop, get out, identify and remonstrate with the driver. All the rest of the way to school I silently compose speeches of controlled fury and coruscating contempt, at which lorry driver bursts into tears, falls to his knees and begs my forgiveness.

Think the better of it on the way back, however. Know full well that the person most likely to burst into tears in such a situation would be myself. Will instead soothe myself with cup of tea.

On arriving home, however, remember that we have run out of tea, sugar and milk – evidence of impartial ineptitude on my part. Not on Spouse's, however. Oh no. He is too grand to shop, although I notice he often manages to force himself into the odd off-licence on the way home. On the rare occasions when he condescends to accompany us to the supermarket, he rails against supermarkets, the standardisation of produce, the triumph of the bland and mass-produced, and the ruin of the individual small shop.

Though I agree with him in theory, feel sure that it would be I who had to slog round the individual small shops, weighed down with carrier bags full of cannon-balls.

Trees have organised their lives much better, I feel. Nobody could expect a tree to go shopping three or four times a week even if it was female. Wonder if I really tried hard, whether I could develop a tap root. And I'd be looking my best just now, new young leaves and blossom tossing about no matter how old and wrinkled my trunk. Knowing my luck, though, there'd be plenty of male dogs about, making straight for my defenceless bole.

Comfort myself with hot Ribena, and since I am in rare mood of feminist rage, ring Alice. She confirms that all we need is a few test-tubes of sperm and we could convert ourselves to a new single-sex species overnight. We share a delectable few minutes trying to decide on the best way to wipe out men. Suggest we force them to shop till they drop.

'OK, but what about Henry?'

Assure Alice that Henry could, if removed from the influence of this macho society, grow up into a graceful gardener, chef or monk.

'He could roam round in a wild life park,' suggests Alice. 'Like Longleat, you know. And women could drive past slowly in closed cars to show their daughters the last surviving specimen.'

At the thought of this sad destiny for my darling son, the ideal of a female-only mistress race begins to pall, and I ring off with specious expressions of solidarity.

Cannot decide whether to go shopping to put off having to get to grips with Bonkbuster, or sit down at word-processor to postpone having to go shopping.

'So: aren't you dazzled, Miss Hoddle, by Paris?' cried Percy Houseboy, flinging his arms about in rapture. 'The elegance, the style, the shops! Have you been ravished by the Rue de Rivoli?'

Fanny shook her head.

'Shops are of no interest to me,' she insisted. 'I would sooner sit on a mountain peak, any day, and admire the glories of nature.'

'Then come with us to Switzerland!' cried Houseboy generously. 'I'm sure Lucien and I would be delighted to offer you our protection, and in return you might manage the odd bit of ironing or sewing, perhaps?'

'Sod that for a lark!' cried Fanny, and astonished her companions by dealing the café table such a blow with her tiny fist that it instantly splintered into smithereens upon the floor.

sixty-six

JEREMY D'ARCY RINGS UP to ask how the Bonkbuster is going, and hopes that Fanny is experiencing a wide range of sexual adventures. Assure him that she is. Cannot face telling him that she has somehow got herself into the company of two homosexual poets and is planning to travel with them to what one vainly hopes will be the licentious stews of Switzerland. In fact, Fanny has not enjoyed a sexual adventure for months, and even then it was with a Scotsman.

Still, that's better going than most of us. Saw a report recently that men are not the swashbuckling lotharios they pretended to be back in the days of the Shere Hite Report. Mind you, they might just be lying, nowadays, about the modesty and moderation of their experience as it is now apparently chic to be celibate. Perhaps Fanny is a heroine for our times after all.

Fanny perused the menu without much understanding. Percy Houseboy instantly observed her embarrassment.

'Let me order for you, my dear.' He turned to the hovering garçon and, pausing only to sweep an appreciative glance over the youth's tight black brocade waistcoat, he launched into what sounded to Fanny like a torrent of incomprehensible Gallic syllables: 'Rognons d'Artagnan Poêlé aux Cravats, Queue de Dôle Farci aux Regrets Paysanne, et Filet de Gilet Rôti aux Epaules Depardieu . . . and, let me see, vegetables . . . Laitues de Mon Moulin, I think, avec Disparges and Frites Absolues.'

Why could I not have married Raymond Blanc? Or even Clement Freud?

. . . 'My compliments to the chef,' sighed Percy Houseboy, wiping the last morsels of the Poire d'Homs Pleins de Promesse de l'Orient from his lips. 'In fact, let's invite him to share a glass of this very fresh young Côte de Burberry.' Lucien conveyed as much to the garçon, who disappeared obediently.

Fanny burped discreetly into the tiny hankie tatted for her by her Great Aunt Flo in her last days, when, immobilised by her goitre, she had sat out in the sun on her granite doorstep at Grinnershaw. This French food was right queer. She had had to slip her rognons secretly into a nearby aspidistra. But when the swing doors burst open and a dashing, nay daemonic figure in a long white apron and carrying a meat-cleaver bore down upon them, she felt her spirits revive a little.

'My dear fellow!' cried Percy Houseboy, 'You are a genius of the table. You cannot imagine the effect of your alchemical arts upon a palate insulted, in its early years, by bread and dripping in a prep school in the shadow of Much Lovelock. Allow me to propose your health.'

Lucien attempted to translate, and while he listened, the chef's enormous black eyes roved incessantly over Fanny's face, and he feverishly fingered his chopper.

'In fact,' Percy continued, 'will you not join us? It is late: your labours must be over. I can see you are charmed by the fine profile of our young companion Miss Hoddle . . .'

The chef seized Fanny's hand and lifted it to his lips.

'Mademoiselle,' he whispered, 'I h'admire you h'exceedingly, but I h'am en ce moment wrestlingue wiz a pig's cheek. Latair I shall be onchonted to convey to you ze Room Sairvice wiz my h'own 'ands – you must taste my Rochers aux Amandes, Mademoiselle.'

And with a burning glance, as of passions almost boiling over, he strode back to his pig's cheek.

'Well, he's certainly got the hots for you, dearie,' remarked Percy with a soupçon of malice. Fanny blushed and shrugged.

'But I don't even know his name,' she murmured, her kidneys somersaulting strangely beneath her modest gaberdine.

''E is Franco Bolli,' explained Lucien. ''Is fazzair was Italien, but 'iz muzzair was Franche. 'Is Moules Bolognese is something special.' Fanny shuddered in anticipation.

Feel hungry. Go to the kitchen and open fridge. Bit of a comedown after the Hôtel Rancide. Sausages old enough to be sitting up, nay perhaps walking. Satisfy myself with Coco

Pops, though suspect, like Shere Hite, they may be of enduring interest only as an anagram.

sixty-seven

Fanny paced nervously up and down in her modest bedroom in the Hôtel Rancide. What had the daemonic chef Franco Bolli really meant when he said, 'I will wiz my h'own 'ands bring you ze Room Sairvice'? Though it was past midnight, the clatter of plates still drifted up from the kitchen courtyard below and through the blistered wooden slats of her shutters Fanny thought she could occasionally hear his voice, but if indeed it was he, what strange bellows were his ejaculations!

'Merde alors!'

Mère Dolor, *thought Fanny, that must mean Mother of Sorrows. She supposed that, for the Latin race, cookery and religion were very closely linked. Eventually the noise subsided somewhat, and every sinew in Fanny's body thrilled at the brisk knock on her door.*

'Who is it?' she called tremulously.

'Eet ees I, Franco!' was the rumbling reply.

She opened the door, and there he stood: hair wild tangles, dark stubble shadowing his majestic chin, and a tray in his hand.

'I 'ave brought you my rocks of h'almond,' he announced, entering the room and placing the tray on a nearby table. 'H'and h'also, a bouteille of champagne.'

He seized the bottle masterfully and, with a light pressure from his strong thumbs, the cork shot off with a loud pop and a fizzing foam exploded into the glasses.

'To your beauté, Mademoiselle 'Oddle,' he murmured. Their glasses clinked, their eyes met, Fanny sipped her champagne gingerly, and sneezed when it tickled her nose.

''Ow delicieuse you are!' breathed Franco. 'I must at least kiss you —' and seizing her roughly, he pressed her to his lips.

At last, thought Fanny, her heart beating wildly beneath her Gritlock and Theakston liberty bodice, here it is. Batter my heart, Oh Franco, grill me, poach me, fry me, kiss me till I boil over, Maestro! But at the conclusion of his kiss, Franco Bolli moved away from her with a regretful bow.

'Hélas, Mademoiselle!' he sighed. 'Delectable h'as you h'are, I am sorry I cannot perform ze rites of Venus wiz you: I am sufferingue from h'an h'infectious h'outbreak of Pinot Noir.'

Fanny's heart smote her. But if rejections were in order, she was not to be outdone.

'Moi aussie je swee un peu mallard,' she sighed, clutching her brow in feigned agony. 'Pas ce soir, sherry, j'ai un Maigret.'

Oh hell. Rise from word-processor and seek refuge in the biscuit barrel. Why can't poor Fanny get laid? Why don't I consign her to a convent and have done with it? And if she can't manage it in Paris, what hopes for the Bernese Oberland?

'Mummee! Where's your nail-varnish remover?'

Marvel at the thought that I might once have painted my nails, and instruct Harriet to look in the bathroom cabinet, which is not so much childproof as child-friendly. A few moments later it occurs to me to wonder why she wants it. Amble to her room, following the stink of acetate. Find Harriet frozen in horror beside her dressing-table.

'Oh sorry Mummy I spilled it!'

The hitherto-varnished surface of the dressing-table is now befouled with a horrid roughened whiteness, as if bats have been roosting above it for years. Harriet bursts into tears.

'I've killed my dressing-table, Mummy!'

Enquire why she wanted my nail-varnish remover in the first place. She informs me between sobs it was because she had varnished Ken's bum. Observe Ken, the male Barbie, sporting red *derrière* fashionable with certain monkeys when sexually receptive. Feel I ought to rebuke Harriet for stupidity and carelessness, but never liked dressing-table anyway (unwanted present from Great Aunt Elspeth: huge, ugly and gloomy, rather like its donor).

'It's all my fault! Waaaaaa!'

'No, it's my fault for letting you have the nail varnish. I'm just a hopeless mother.'

'No you're *not*! Don't *say that*! I love you even though you've got old hands!'

Harriet clings to me. Promise her that we can sand down and revarnish dressing-table, Ken's bottom and, if necessary, my embarrassing old hands.

sixty-eight

SPOUSE INVITED TO DELIVER a lecture in Amsterdam. In English. How jolly polyglot the Dutch are. In the tradition of Erasmus, of course. Did I dream it, or is there a range of shaving products called Erasmus? Oh well. Why shouldn't he go the way of Milton, Marvell and Earl Grey?

Surprisingly, Spouse proposes that I should accompany him and make a weekend in Amsterdam of it. Hesitate. Attracted by the thought of Van Gogh, and teetering old seventeenth-century houses, but increasingly haunted by hitherto dormant fear of flying. Thank Spouse for offer, but must reluctantly decline as it is my duty to take care of the children.

'Oh, dump 'em on Robbie Coltrane,' says Spouse – a malicious reference to Mrs Body, to whom he appeals the minute she walks in the door.

'Oh yes of course Mr Domum they'll be no trouble at all bless their hearts you go off and have a lovely weekend together,' she winks, the lewd old bawd.

Express polite reluctance to impose on her, though have cheerfully done so a hundred times when not threatened with flying machine.

The die is cast, however. Or should I say Never Say Die? Distracted briefly by arrival of junk mail, viz, subscription to *Which? Way to Health*. 'Read our investigations into the NHS, seafood contamination, artificial sweeteners . . .' And condoms: 'Our unique set of tests reveals all.' Oh well. Death in air crash would at least end anxiety over health.

Make sure Will is in Important Drawer. By some miracle passports are also there. Was hoping they'd be lost. Tempted to lose them immediately, possibly on top of Unimportant Wardrobe, but decide I must submit to Fate. Probably greater risk of death by staying at home in Rusbridge, especially now gardening has become unavoidable.

Switch on radio only to hear man talking about Lockerbie. Switch off again. Have a bath. Shampoo says Wash'n'Go. Sounds apocalyptic, a bit like Drink and Depart. Wonder if Aunt Elspeth could manage another stroke by Friday.

Raid fridge, as usual in times of crisis. Help myself to juice, then notice it is called Five Alive. Is this reassuring, or not? Which five? Are Spouse and I among them? Recall recent air disaster in Holland and wonder if there is something wrong with Amsterdam airport, of which our flight is to be fatal proof.

Children resist weekend at Mrs Body's, despite reminders of Battenberg cake.

'She washed my neck last time!' cries Harriet indignantly. Bribe children with promise of presents from Holland, make peanut butter sandwiches for them, and sentimentally stroke their heads, which shine with a strange poignant radiance.

'Gerroff, Mum!'

Imagine Henry in middle age, waxing nostalgic with his wife, the daughter-in-law I shall never meet. (Perhaps some comfort in air crash after all.)

'I remember her making us peanut butter sandwiches,' sighs the middle-aged Henry, 'the day before. And she stroked my head and I said Gerroff Mum. Do you think she Must Have Known?'

'Oh, do shut up about your bloody mother,' snaps daughter-in-law. 'You're obsessed.'

'Don't go, Mummy, don't go!' Harriet bursts into my reverie and hugs me with sympathetic dread. 'I shall miss you so much, like I miss Grandpa and the gerbil!'

Point out, not without quiver, that she has enrolled me within the ranks of the deceased and this is precipitate. Offer to let her help me pack. My clothes hanging in the wardrobe already look forlorn. Harriet tries on my earrings and asks if she may have them now as she can't wait till I'm dead.

Lie awake wondering how *Which?* tested its condoms, and rehearsing my funeral. Fear Tom will not be allowed to jump down into my grave, now he is a married man. Oh well. Would prefer Viking funeral really: floating down the Piddle in blazing punt.

At 3 a.m., Spouse suddenly wakes up, rushes to the bathroom and much to my surprise and delight, is violently sick.

'I'm sure it was those bloody prawns I had in the Faculty canteen,' he groans greenly. Thank God we hadn't read *Which? Guide to Contaminated Seafood* or he'd never have touched them. Promise to summon doctor, apologise to Amsterdam, and nurse him tenderly all weekend if he will cancel trip. He agrees like a shot.

'To tell you the truth,' confesses Spouse on Sunday evening, risking a boiled egg, 'I was dreading that damned lecture.'

sixty-nine

HALF-TERM – LATEST IN series of education-free days since Easter: Baker Days (as they used quaintly to be known), May Day (ditto), and then a day when a mobile classroom was hoisted into place over the roof of the school and the little darlings had a day off so they wouldn't be in the way. Instead they were in the way at home.

'Mum please can we have a video?'

'*No!*' . . . Although we all know what videos mean. Ninety minutes' peace. But Henry and Harriet are showing worrying symptoms of APE syndrome: Acquiring Possessions Everyday so . . . 'No! But if you're good we'll go to Rusbridge Street Fair.'

'Will there be stalls?'

Stalled by this cunning enquiry. Of course there will be stalls: a street fair being the High Mass of Market Forces.

'Well, probably, but there'll be really exciting things like conjurors and clowns and er . . . musicians.'

'Can we have some money to spend? Pleeease mummy? If you let us have a pound each today we won't have any more pocket money till the end of the year.'

'Julian has a pound every Saturday,' mutters Henry darkly. This *sacra conversazione* interrupted by arrival from London of Spouse, who has been away for a couple of days researching in a library. Allegedly.

'British Rail have stopped calling us passengers!' he explodes wrathfully. 'We're *customers* now. Can you believe it? "Will customers for Oxford please change at Didcot." Customers, my arse!'

Children titter at this reference to the paternal fundament.

Wonder if privatisation of BR will lead to that Holy Grail, a Choice of Services, i.e. white linen tablecloths, drawn blinds and string quartets in the Executive Lounge but leg-irons, stinking pallets and a bucket of pigswill for the rest of us.

Inform Spouse we are about to patronise Rusbridge Street Fair and invite him to join us. Not bloody likely is the elegant reply, and besides, it is his melancholy duty to watch the Test Match.

En route, remind children – or perhaps I should say potential customers – that we are not going to town to buy things but to have a Rewarding Experience.

'Buying things is a rewarding experience!' shouts Harriet, accurately, I fear. Detect myself hock-deep in priggery and recall previous occasions when I have shopped till I swooned in a orgy of acquisition. Console myself with the vague memory that St Augustine was something of a happy shopper before achieving sanctity.

'In the old days,' I announce as we stride purposefully towards the fair, 'fairs were places to enjoy yourself. They had jugglers and fire-eaters and servants went there to be hired and –'

'Oh, good!' interrupts Harriet. 'Can I have a servant?'

Remind her that she already has one, i.e. me.

'Mum?' Henry tugs at my sleeve going past Woolworth's. 'Can we go into Woolworth's just for a minute they've got this ace thing called a Blurp Blaster it's like a horrible monster-like head thing and you squeeze it and this blob thing shoots out of its mouth as if it's being sick.'

Experience deep desire to be transported to Arcadian sheep-fair, *à la Winter's Tale*. Although recall Autolycus was a dab hand at a rip-off.

What did Perdita say? 'Welcome to our shearing'? Now it's Come and Get Fleeced. Rusbridge pedestrian precinct, often deserted except for the odd dodgy character loitering (pederastrian precinct they should call it) now decked out with stalls selling every necessity of life from huge inflatable hammers to small semi-precious stones suitable for insertion into nose. First, one assumes, nose must be pierced. Painful, no doubt, but presumably making it easier to pay through, a desirable facility in *fin-de-siècle* Britain, and indeed fin-de-sickle Russia.

Stand on edge of huge crowd watching clown. Hope for rewarding pastoral experience but children grumble that they cannot see properly. Start to feel giddy and agoraphobic so rush off into nearest shop and buy Harriet magic wand adorned with nice medieval-faced golden sun. Henry demands bloodshot eyeball in plastic or Snot fair. Reluctantly acquiesce, though aware I am fatally going back on my word.

Within five minutes Harriet has lost the magic wand, though, inevitably, bloodshot eyeball still with us. Snot fair indeed.

seventy

'MUMMEEEEE! OW OW OW! 'T'URTS!'

Two a.m. It is Spouse's turn, but he pretends to be asleep. Place the soles of my feet on his back and shove, like young cuckoo. Spouse exits at speed and slouches off with dark oaths. He returns almost immediately and falls back into bed with satisfied thud.

'She wants you. It's women's troubles.'

Harriet writhing about in her bed: putting it on a bit, I hope. God knows she's seen her father do it often enough.

'Hurts! In my pee place! Ow!'

Suggest that a trip to the bathroom will sort her out, but 'Pee burning! Hot hot hot! Ow! Wish I'd never been born!' Thrush? Cystitis? Vaguely remember reading in one of Alice's feminist health handbooks that thrush can be treated with yogurt or diluted vinegar. Go down to fridge but find only a pot of Aero chocolate pud. Doubt whether applying that would be either effective or aesthetically pleasing. Prepare bowl of warm water and add a few drops of tarragon vinegar. Haunted by the conviction that I do not know what I am doing, but cleverly refrain from adding salt, pepper or mustard.

Harriet fast asleep, so leave bowl of warm water at her bedside and return to my own. Sleep eludes me for another three hours. Bonkbuster is stalled: heroine apparently unable to cross Alps. Am just drifting off when Harriet jumps on my head shouting, 'Mummy! I've knocked a bowl of water over! You shouldn't have left it there you idiot!'

Pee still hot, so doctor's surgery next port of call. Waiting room well supplied with old copies of *Hello* magazine and tea machine. Slurp endless cups of tea and gawp at photos of celebrities glowing with shared domestic bliss. Most have since divorced if not killed each other. At last doctor sees Harriet, gives us a small bottle and asks if she could provide a specimen before leaving.

Take up least favourite position: head down loo, holding specimen bottle in place, but it is like trying to get blood out of stone.

'Come on, darling! Widdly widdly widdly! Fountains! Torrents! Rivers! Streams!'

'Can't! No, wait, Mummy! It's coming . . . No it's not.'

'Well, get off a minute, then! I'm absolutely bursting!'

Half an hour passes, during which I pee five times because of all the tea, but Harriet, despite drinking three glasses of water, can only produce a tiny drop suggestive of gnat spit. Receptionist says it will do, and we escape through torrential rain. Halfway home Harriet suddenly cries, 'Stop the car I'm desperate!'

Happen to be passing garage. Rush in, purchase packet of unleaded Eccles cakes to establish customer status and then ask to use loo.

'Sorry, Madam, it is out of order.'

Rush out again, Harriet swearing vilely. 'It's like a horrible dream, Mummy!'

Propose that she pees on the kerbside grass. After all she is only a child.

'Never! People in cars going past could see my botty!'

Have vague memory of Renaissance astronomer Tycho de Brahe who died of a burst bladder because he was at a feast where the guest of honour was too important for people to Be Excused from his presence. Turn off main road at first opportunity, but find ourselves in residential cul de sac. Tempted to evacuate Harriet on someone's Cistus, or perhaps Cytisus, and do a runner. Woman taking dog for a walk is doing just that.

'Oh lucky *dog*!' moans Harriet. Execute fourteen-point turn at speed and scorch off across main road and down promising dark lane. Blessed hedge appears. Stop car and we both pee in shadow thereof, howling with relief. Still raining torrentially – helps somehow. Harriet remarks that God is flushing it away for us, isn't that nice of him?

'It's not fair!' she cries later. 'Why can't we wee-wee like men? They can wee standing up as if they're not doing it really.'

'I expect it's because God was a man,' I sigh.

'Or a dog,' ponders Harriet. 'GOD is DOG backwards, have you ever noticed, Mummy? And dogs are sweet aren't they? And lovely like God.'

'Er . . . yes.' Unequal to theological debate, somehow.

'Well *can we have one then*? Not a big one like Mrs Body's Bonzo just little like Twinkle that one Aunt Elspeth used to have. A terror.'

'A terrier, you mean. No, sorry. Absolutely not.'

'Can I have the day off school then? After all I am really –'

Hastily agree. Anything rather than dog. Quail at thought of having to organise evacuations of domestic pets when clearly unable to coordinate our own.

seventy-one

HIGH SUMMER, JUDGING BY the weeds and the smell o'th'dustbin. Watch Test Match on TV with sound turned down, and listen to ball-by-ball commentary: Bill Frindall totting up, Brian Johnstone tittering, and Trevor Bailey tut-tutting. Suddenly a reference to Border reminds me that I must go out and water mine. Children excited by the hose.

'Spray me, Mummy! Oh please!' shrieks Harriet.

'No – let me spray her! Oh go on, Mum!'

Suspect these utterances reveal what male biologist would call innate sexual differences. Sadly contemplate what I can only call bad bedding.

'I think my blasted nicotianas are *shrinking*,' I lament.

Spouse emerges, exhausted by day's play, and abominates selectors.

'Daddy! Mummy says her knickers are shrinking!' shouts Harriet.

Spouse offers the opinion that it is my bum that is expanding. Harriet enquires of him urgently if he will still love me if I get as fat as Grotbags.

'I suppose so,' sighs Spouse morosely. If he were a plant, he would be a Douglas Fir. Indignantly point out nicotianas, which have shrunk four inches since they were planted weeks ago. Spouse blames slugs.

'Ugh I hate slugs!' cries Harriet. 'They look like poos walking about!'

Have always hesitated over slug pellets since I read somewhere that mice eat the poisoned slugs and owls eat the poisoned mice and go sterile. Spouse enquires What about supper as he suspects it is my turn. Go indoors and open fridge. Fly flies out: always a difficult moment. Four uncovered dishes in there: ham, potato salad, taramasalata and fruit salad, on all of which I suspect fly has pooed.

'How about ham or tara and potato salad?'

'Fine.'

Think I will stick to toast and Marmite, myself. Children sup as usual on pieces of fish pulverised and reassembled into shapes of fishes – a monument to man's pointless meddling with nature. Spouse alone will ingest the fly-poo: perhaps nature's chance for revenge.

After dark, go out with torch to inspect nicotianas. Crowds of snails swarming all over them, including baby snails with exquisite tiny pink shells. Snails more endearing than slugs. Possibly because they carry their house around with them, run indoors and slam the door at the first hint of visitors. Admire them with considerable pang of fellow-feeling, then go and tell Spouse I cannot contemplate slug pellets.

'They carry their houses with them?' he echoes mockingly. 'Well, try thinking of them as New Age travellers. That should do the trick.' And he unfurls the newspaper with a contemptuous flourish.

Appalled. Hope fly-poo makes him feel really ill. Have always felt sneaking sympathy with New Age travellers, and wish I was grand landowner who could offer them convenient park with freshwater spring and reed-bed loos, though have been informed by Spouse that if I was really a grand landowner I would think differently. Spouse groans at something in the paper. Gently enquire what.

'Oh this confounded Is Major Too Weak debate. Of course the bloke's weak, that's why they chose him, isn't it?' Enquire why. 'Well after Herself bossing us all about for ten years what they wanted was the sort of bloke who'd share his sandwiches with you at Lord's. But now they think they'd be better off with a Führer after all.'

Inform him I would rather have a weak government any day, and as few laws as possible, so we could all muddle along sensibly on our own.

'Yes, well, you would think that,' sighs Spouse. Hope fly-poo kills him. 'But do you really want me never to roar at the children again?'

Confess I do depend heavily on his ability to frighten the children, and secretly hope fly-poo does not have too adverse an effect after all. Go out with torch again and, using tablespoon, fling snails and slugs over fence. Not into the Twills' garden: slug pellets applied in neat military rows there, so the molluscs can die tidily. No: my slugs and snails soar westwards to a new and happy life in old Mrs Bailey's neglected wilderness. Do not wish to poison snails, but do not want them rampaging around my back yard.

So despite sneaking sympathy for New Age travellers, I seem to be a closet NIMBY after all. Would also, were I England selector, go out after dark and wield the giant tablespoon with gusto.

seventy-two

GOWER SELECTED FOR SUMMER holiday: a cricketo-politico gesture of solidarity, according to Spouse. We are getting a little hopelessly nostalgic, Spouse and I, as cricket selectors.

'So,' I conclude, 'we're also going to get a Jack Russell terrier, I suppose. But what do you want for Sunday lunch? Lamb or Beefy?'

'Both'em,' grunts Spouse.

'You're stuck in the past. What I say is, give the young chaps a chance.'

'Yes, well, you would.'

An icicle of fear descends through my guts. What does Spouse mean by that? Something sinister, or just the usual contempt?

We are watching *Lady Chatterley's Lover*, as a kind of nostalgic duty, since we were the generation that read foreign-printed editions under the bedclothes.

'My problem,' admits Spouse, 'is that I can't tell whether we're watching Lady Chatterley or the Lions versus the All Blacks.'

We conclude in the end that there are more fouls, and filthier rucks and mauls, in Lady C., but that Gavin Hastings is a lot sexier than the gamekeeper.

'Well,' observes Spouse after watching another frenzied bout of pneumatic buttocking, 'it's encouraging to see a bloke who's even worse at it than I am.'

Feel quite fond of Spouse for a split second and admit that it all seems lacking in oomph, compared to how it was under the blankets, long ago.

'Ludicrous project anyway,' sneers Spouse. 'At least Lawrence managed to mention the unmentionable. Unfortunately for Ken Russell it's still the unshowable.'

Wonder for a moment if Ken Russell is any relation of Jack. Spouse yawns, and speculates whether film rights to my Bonkbuster might one day be bought by Ken Russell – if I ever bestir myself to finish it.

Uneasily aware that I haven't touched it for weeks. Make my excuses and go to study. Peruse Bonkbuster. Bonk-quotient alarmingly low. Feel I must rouse myself to new heights of erotic endeavour, but heroine is on train in Alps with a pair of gay poets, Lucien Penible and Percy Houseboy. Am about to whisk her peremptorily to Bernese Oberland and foul encounter in pinewood near Faulensee with muscular shepherd, when distracted by small but delightfully recherché guidebook to Gower. It includes details of Gower's own lingo, preserved till the end of the last century by its relative isolation as a sort of haemorrhoid hanging off the bum of Wales.

Bubback apparently means a scarecrow or dull person, *nipparty* means perky and *rining* means mooching or scrounging. There is also a most interesting essay on marine life.

Washed up after a storm you will find several kinds of *Jellyfish*; the blue-edged oval *membranes* of the *By-the-Wind Sailor*, *Heart Urchins* and the *testis* of *Sea Urchins*: the horny black *egg cases* of the *Skate*, the softer transparent ones of the

Dogfish called respectively Fisherman's and Mermaid's Purses . . .

Fall into contemplative extasie. Why, when it comes to lidderature I be a mere bubback, theze yere ecological guidebooks be more poetical than I. I be fit fer nawt zave rining. Stare out of the window into the dark and pick my nose. Suddenly hitherto unsuspected bogey, like huge jelly-fish, adheres to my fingertip and insists on making a public appearance. Thank God, or rather Mrs Body, that there are paper hankies on my desk, not like last time this happened: in the doctor's waiting room. Never pick your nose in public. You could stir up a hornet's nest.

Wish my heroine could search for mermaid's purses and collect the horny black egg cases of the skate, her skirts tucked up to reveal her shining limbs, until a swarthy gatherer of laverbread sweeps her into his marine embrace, and they couple in the rockpools to the distant booming of the surf. Alas, fear this will prove rather difficult to arrange in Switzerland.

Spouse comes suddenly into study, looking unusually nipparty, and astonishes me by casting aside his habitual sloth and pleasuring me upon my desk. Enquire afterwards whether his libido was stimulated by Lady Chatterley, to which he replies No: Gavin Hastings.

Lying in bed later Spouse has even worse attack of nostalgia and explains why Lady C. is so dull. 'I blame the selectors,' quoth he. 'Cast W. G. Grace as the gamekeeper, Vita Sackville-West as Connie and Peter May as Sir Clifford, and you might be getting somewhere.' Cannot but agree.

seventy-three

BROAD DAYLIGHT IN BEDROOM: open eye: 5 a.m. Sink back into delightful dream: discover previously unsuspected Georgian wing in our 1920s semi. Plan to establish elegant new study in large panelled room. Brilliant daylight prises open eyelids again, but still only 6.25 a.m. Wonderful summer mornings. Return voluptuously to unconsciousness. Open eyes again. Oh horror! It is 8.30. Have overslept.

Hurtle from bed and wake Spouse with demented yell. Rush through house pulling on most of yesterday's clothes. Find children half-dressed, watching TV, and scream that Daddy wants them in the car in three minutes. Then start frenzied clear-up as it is Thursday and Mrs Body will arrive at any moment. There are so many things She Must Never Know.

Pick up dirty clothes and hurl them into laundry basket, recalling Betty Boothroyd's recent revelation on *Desert Island Discs* that she always hung up her clothes the moment she took them off, fastidiously brushing the collars of the jackets, etc. Amazed that people manage to find time to brush so many unusual things, when it's a battle for me to manage even my hair. Feel sure I saw hairbrush in washing-up bowl, so run downstairs. Suddenly notice relics of Indian take-away in oven, abandoned two days earlier. Catch sight of my reflection in dark glass of oven door. Look like sinister scarecrow. Must brush hair before Mrs Body arrives. Cannot find hairbrush so run to Harriet's room and attempt to use Sindy comb one and a half inches long. Lose comb in thickest thickets.

Hear Mrs Body's key in front door, below. Kitchen a lost cause but I must at least do something about the bathroom floor. Lock myself therein, pick up three befouled towels and fold hypocritically on wooden towel rail, which collapses at this outrage owing to failure of glue in joints. Reassemble towel rail, pinching palm with brief suppressed howl. Then award myself a few moments of calm on the loo.

Suddenly notice that three Sindies are lying in the bath, mummified in loo roll and scattered with talc. Some funeral game. In clearing up the mess somehow I get my shoulder under shelf unit and accidentally lift one end of it off the wall, causing toothbrushes, deodorant, Spouse's shaving things, shampoo, etc, etc to slide off the edge and dive into loo. Paralysed for a moment with hands full and shoulder still under shelving, convinced that any move I make will result in final disintegration of bathroom and perhaps also sanity.

Finally shrug off shelving and gaze balefully into loo, where Spouse's shaving brush is swimming about like aquatic mammal. Realise with horrid pang that I had not had time to flush loo. No rubber gloves in bathroom so trip downstairs necessary.

'Good morning, dear!' cries Mrs Body. 'You forgot to put the bags out, look, it's Thursday.'

Oh hell. Dustbin men have tiptoed past in the dazzling dawn whilst I dreamt of secret wing of house. Wish I lived there.

What's more, dustbin contains chicken carcass, already pongy. Cannot bear thought of it hanging around for another week. Seize Indian take-away debris, complete with aluminium foil containers which better women would wash and recycle. Rush out, throw armful of rubbish in bin, then attempt to pull out and secure bag, but its handle is severed by subversive presence within of sharp-edged tin. Rush indoors for new bag.

'Can you manage dear? Shall I give you a hand?'

'Oh, no thanks,' I cry with gay despair, 'it's fine!'

Outside again, manage to insert heavy stinking torn bag into clean one, fasten and carry to car. Sling in back, cursing the fact that it is a Volvo estate and therefore has no decent boot in which to isolate unpleasant cargo – not like Spouse's nice new nippy little Peugeot. Car keys in pocket – amazing concession from gods – so whizz off down country road towards what used to be called The Tip and is now Recycling Centre.

Uneasily aware that my bag contains metal, paper and teabags as well as the stinking cadaver of a fowl. Recall how Tom used to segregate, rationalise and recycle all our refuse. Wonder how he ever found the time for all that, let alone adultery with me. Sudden recall that Spouse's shaving brush, etc, is still in loo, and that Mrs Body must have found it all by now.

Somehow it is almost a relief when car shudders to a halt in isolated spot. Have run out of petrol – *again*. Lean head against steering wheel. Sindy comb falls out of hair. Wish I was Betty Boothroyd. Or even Betty Boop.

seventy-four

PARENT'S EVENING AT RUSBRIDGE Primary. Harriet's teacher is Miss Murgatroyd, a delightful young woman with slinky hair and many bracelets which draw attention to the slim perfection of her brown arms. Spouse clearly glad I bullied him into coming, asks abstruse questions about the National Curriculum. Miss Murgatroyd waves her brown arms about whilst explaining it all. Try to listen, but am distracted by the envious thought that I never had arms that were slim or brown let along both.

Our daughter's school report is a mystery, however. 'Harriet is a pleasant, polite little girl who is always eager to please.' Amazed that Miss Murgatroyd has failed to notice that Harriet is in fact a foul-mouthed termagant. In car on way home, wonder about origin of termagant. Sounds like a sea-bird. Murgatroyd, on the other hand, would be a very good name for a toad.

Arrive home to find children avidly watching video *Batman Returns*, which babysitter Tracey has brought, despite its being a '15 and over', and therefore much too adult for our little innocents. Cast anxious glance at screen where Michelle Pfeiffer, dressed in skin-tight black patent cat-suit, is inflicting pain on a man wearing a fetishistic mask. Spouse immediately announces he will watch it with them, no need to fuss, and a cup of tea would be nice.

Help Tracey to clear away greasy relics of children's TV dinner, but on way to kitchen notice Answerphone is blinking.

'Hello, dearrr? . . . Is it the machine . . .? Och, you know I hate these things. I just rang to tell Gordon that his Auntie Kitty has died, poor thing, but she was ninety-five, it was a blessed relief really. The funeral's next Wednesday. I'll tell you the details when you ring me back.'

Interesting that Aunt Elspeth assumes that Spouse is too grand to listen to his own Answerphone. Spouse himself too grand to put on kettle. If only I could write best-selling Bonkbuster I'd be mega-grand: I'd go and live in a tower by the sea in faery lands forlorn and sod the lot of them.

Make pot of tea, however, since I quite fancy one myself, and that's what he relies on, the lazy bastard. Tracey does the washing-up but I have to ask her to do the drying-up and putting-away. 'Would you mind . . .? Thanks so much.' Decide I am constitutionally unsuited to be an employer, perpetually guilty and grovelling. Perhaps I should go on an assertiveness training course, as suggested by Elaine-over-the-road. Have not seen her recently, and fear she may have got involved with another dismally unsuitable bloke.

Inform Spouse of the death of his Auntie Kitty, to which he replies 'Who?', never taking his eyes off Michelle Pfeiffer for an instant. Sigh and withdraw to kitchen, where I grudgingly pay Tracey, knowing the mess the children's rooms will be in as she always somehow inspires them to acts of feral abandon. After she departs I go upstairs to discover depressing confirmation of my intuition. Harriet's dressing-table is covered with pools of Coke, exploded teabags and uncooked pasta. Am unable to enter Henry's room owing to something heavy having fallen down behind the door.

Spouse comes upstairs calling, 'Did you say Antiquity had died?' Evidently alarmed as he is a historian and dedicates all his intellectual energies to resuscitating the past. Spouse relieved to discover it was only his Auntie Kitty. Last time we saw her was in 1974 and she was rather a bad-tempered old trout even then.

'Still, I suppose you'd better go to the funeral,' sighs her devoted nephew.

Express outrage and incredulity that Spouse considers he is too grand even for funerals. He explains, with audible capitals, that next Wednesday will be Absolutely Impossible as he is due to give a Public Lecture at a conference. Argue half-heartedly for a while, then begin to think I might quite enjoy a nice peaceful funeral in Yorkshire, where Auntie Kitty spent the last decades of her trouthood.

Harriet runs in, hurls herself into my arms and shouts, 'Can I have a unicorn or a mermaid, Mummy? For having a good report?'

Henry, not to be out-grabbed, roars, 'And can I have a dinosaur?'

Manage to avoid committing myself to provide my children with mythological and extinct beasts – cleverest thing I have done all day.

Fall exhausted into bed and am annoyed to find that Spouse is intent on amorous rites – twice in a fortnight. Whatever is the matter with the man? This Michelle Pfeiffer has got to be stopped.

seventy-five

HENRY, HAVING SAVED UP a bit of pocket money, buys himself a plastic badminton set. Am congratulating him on acquiring two rackets, a shuttlecock and a plastic carrying case for £1.99 when I notice the sinister legend: Made in China. Dread to think what working conditions or environmental pollution might have been involved in its manufacture, and wish it had been expensive and Made in England.

'I want to play bagminton!' cries Harriet eagerly.

'Ugh! Not her!' roars Henry. 'She's useless! I want you to play, Mum!'

'I can't! I've got to get ready for the funeral!'

'You bastard!' cries Harriet at her brother, striking him loudly over the head with a box of Jungle Fever Tear'n'Draw Recycled Paper Roll. 'I can't help it! I'm only little!'

'Ouch! Mum! She hit me!'

'Ow! He kicked me, Mummy! I'll kill you for that!'

Feel that life consists of a tidal wave of exclamation marks, ready to sweep over me and drown me, rather like that terrifying advert for mouth-watering Fruit Opals.

Run upstairs, but children pursue me. Lock myself in bathroom. Fifteen minutes before I have to leave for Aunt Kitty's funeral in Yorkshire and babysitter ten minutes late. Spouse is elsewhere in southern England, delivering an Important Lecture. Somehow nothing I do is deemed important enough to excuse me from attending his aunt's funeral. Never mind.

'Mummee! He hit me with the bagminton racket!'

'She's stamping on my shuttlecock!'

Funeral is assuming a strange attractive glamour. Cannot believe I will be allowed to sit unmolested in quiet pew for half an hour. Still, knowing my luck, Aunt Kitty's coffin lid will be hurled back at a crucial moment, and she will leap up shouting, I fancy a cup of tea, Dulcie! And fetch me my corn plasters, that chiropodist has crippled me!

Rashly promise the children I will play five minutes' badminton with each of them before I go. We play on the front lawn, the better to wait anxiously for the arrival of Tracey Body, who promised faithfully to be here by now, put the children to bed, and protect them from all ill until the arrival home of their father at ten-ish. By which time I shall be approaching that other treat: a night by myself in a B and B in Yorkshire.

Badminton a lot more difficult and tiring than I remember: the thrashing about of arms above head height a deeply irrational activity. Henry swipes shuttlecock into orbit. Leap to return it, badly wrenching shoulder and ricking ankle. Does not matter, though, as it is now Harriet's turn. A much more restful experience for her opponent, as it takes her seven attempts before the bat encounters cock at all. Take advantage of this respite to peer anxiously over hedge, hoping for sight of Tracey.

Behold instead Elaine-over-the-road, looking stunning as usual in dusty pink dress and coral earrings. Complain loudly to her that she is deeply tanned at which she assures me it is out of a bottle, like most of the best things in life, and flourishes a brace of Sancerre, inviting me to join her, insisting the children can play badminton on her lawn instead. Inform her I am about to depart for funeral, as soon as –

Phone rings in deep recess of house – rush to answer it – Tracey in tears at other end – enquire if boyfriend trouble – she says no, it's hay fever, her eyes have closed ub, her dose is ruddig and she is *achoo achoo achoo*, she hates to let me dowd but *achoo*. Assure her she must stay at home and get better, and I didn't want to go to the funeral anyway.

This was a lie, I realise as I go back out into the garden, where Elaine instantly gets to grips with the situation, insists she will babysit, no trouble at all.

'Will you play badminton with us?' roar my frightful offspring, and Elaine elegantly agrees at once, promising them pancakes afterwards. Grab overnight bag gratefully and run to car.

Map of Yorkshire a wonder document: such names. Myth-olmroyd, Heptonstall, Pecket Well Slack, Oughtershaw,

Winksley, Fearby, Eccup. How they conjure up the voice of Fred Trueman, whose eloquence is too contained ever to need exclamation marks. Point old Volvo north, a direction most congenial to it, and also to me, since the sun is never in your eyes. Wallow in prospect of child-free twenty-four hours and bless Elaine aloud. Suspect this trip may put the fun back in funeral.

seventy-six

SPOUSE, CHILDREN AND HOUSEHOLD cares left behind, I drive serenely through, or rather up and down, Yorkshire landscape. A bit like one of those fairground rides. The Yorkshire Dipper. Feel a bit sick, actually.

Stomach uneasy because of earlier part of my treat – bed and fried breakfast, taken *en route*. Have ingested large quantity of pig instead of usual frugal oatcake. Now at every lurch into t'dale I fear my breakfast may be born again. Mrs Bottomley would never have indulged herself like that. What an odd name that women has. Only she could get away with Bottomley. She should be Mrs Topping or Mrs Ripping.

Dream Topping and Absolutely Ripping . . . they sound like villages in the south of England. Except in Dorset, where they get a bit strange, even Papal. Victor Ludorum and Intricate Drivel. Whereas up here the villages are all seized-up machines that need oiling. Crankup. Hurdthorpe. Theakly. Blassett . . . Ah. Here we are at the chapel.

Am pinned into the innermost corner of a pew, my exit cut off by a line of stout aunts. By 'eck, it's 'ot. Phew what a scorcher. Aunt Elspeth ostentatiously prays on arrival: I ostentatiously don't. But within a few bars of 'The Old Rugged Cross' I'm praying all right; praying not to be sick. The organ swings and lurches up and down, like a North Sea coal-barge rising and falling in a heavy swell. Sweat breaks out all over, and I suddenly remember that this too-thick dress is not colour-fast and that, if I ever get out of this alive, I shall have black armpits.

Finally we escape into the fresh air, only to face the second ordeal of standing round the grave whilst the sun hammers down on our heads. 'Dust to dust . . .' Wish he wouldn't mention food. 'Ashes to ashes . . .' Or cricket.

Am embraced afterwards by old rugged aunt who tells me I have Kitty's nose. Forbear to point out that is my Spouse who is a blood-relation of the deceased and I am a mere conjugal adjunct. Annoy myself afterwards by trying to remember what sort of nose Aunt Kitty had, and wondering if she was thought handsome in her youth.

By 3 p.m. I am longing to fly south. Even Leicestershire has acquired a faintly tropical air. I am already homesick for villages in the Present Continuous Tense, like Old Gatting. Or do I mean Gerunds? Gerunds end in ING too. What a shame I did not pay more attention in those grammar lessons thirty years ago. Then I would know what a Gerund was, instead of merely thinking it sounds like Virginia Topping's husband. Gerund Topping, the Member for Much Wapping. ('It never did me any harm.')

Return to Rusbridge to find astonishing sight: Elaine-over-the-road *still there*, nay doing my ironing. Express horror and foreboding.

'Oh, it's all right, Dulcie, only Gordon rang last night to say he wouldn't manage to make it home till today – I think he got pissed actually – he looks a bit fragile.' Televisual cricketing sounds issue from sitting room. 'So I stayed the night, the kids were thrilled. Then today when I got back from taking them to school and your cleaner lady rang to say she couldn't come, so I thought, well, now's my chance to play Mummies and Daddies till Dulcie gets back. Isn't this *adorable!*'

Elaine indicates small dress belonging to Harriet. Express unbounded gratitude and apologise for behaviour of Spouse, but Elaine perversely seems to have loved every minute.

'Henry and Harriet are upstairs tidying their rooms. It's really funny, you ask them to do something and they do it. I'd always thought children would be awkward, but yours are lovely!'

Mind boggles, but suppose that all this is a novelty to Elaine, since she enjoys that blessed state: childless and Spouseless. Of course she is equally a novelty to the children, hence their obedience.

Venture into sitting room where Spouse is watching *The Ashes Regained*, a video of the 1985 series. I missed 1985 owing to the arrival of Harriet. Admire Gower's mysterious beauty, like face of fourteenth-century Florentine angel. Whole thing seems episode from a mythic past when we thrashed Australia and cricket was playful and graceful. Now *Homo Ludens* replaced by *Homo Broodens*.

One glance suffices to inform me that Spouse is so deeply hung-over there is no prospect of a civil word from him, let alone an expression of gratitude for my having buried his aunt. Retire to kitchen to find Elaine has poured Sancerre into two strangely sparkling glasses. V. tempted to have a sex-change so I could marry her instead.

seventy-seven

PHONE CALL FROM MY publisher: a woman called Cleo Goldstone introduces herself as my new editor and informs me that Jeremy D'Arcy has moved on, in tones which discourage me from asking where. Cleo confides that she has been reading the latest bit of Bonkbuster which I sent them and says she loves it, but there is not enough chagrin.

'Chagrin?'

'*Shagging*.'

Recoil, apologising foolishly, and promise to rush her several thousand words of shagging immediately. Then bite lip. Bonkbuster heroine Fanny is marooned in the Bernese Oberland, where shags, even of the ornithological sort, are probably very rare. Still, must do my best, though Spouse has summer school, so childcare is *up* to me as we used to say in the perky old days. The vile modern phrase 'it's down to me', sums up the *fin-de-siècle* depression which prevails. Not enough chagrin? Too much, by heaven.

Children are staring open-mouthed at TV, so tiptoe to study and retrieve Bonkbuster from under pile of drawings of ghosts, corpses and vampires. Can't think why Cleo is so keen on shagging when croaking is what turns the next generation on. Activate word-processor with a sigh, and force my mind to contemplate the erotic potential of Switzerland.

Fanny wandered in the fire woods above Fallenfaul. Lucien and Percy were still dozing back at the Hotel Gastglut. They hardly ever appeared before noon, so Fanny filled her mornings with solitary rambles. But the steep climb up from Schwangern had racked her rococo chest with deep pants. She threw herself down on an immaculate carpet of edelweiss and pulled out her Faustus. *A bare moment had passed when a stout hobnailed boot appeared beside her book.*

'Guten morgen, schone Fraulein!'

[Must check this. My German has lain untouched for thirty years – as perhaps, if I do not get on with it, will Fanny.]

Fanny blinked up at a muscular figure, his naked thighs gleaming below his lederhosen, his blond hair flickering like flames against the sun. [Hope not too Third Reich.] *Slowly, hypnotically, he lowered himself on to his haunches before her. Fanny's senses swam.*

'Or . . .' he hesitated. He had somehow divined her nationality. [i.e., have run out of German:] *'. . . are you perhaps ein goddess? Evenso beautiful do you to me seem. My heart when I behold you out of mein chest jumps. Shall I you the Finsteraarhorn show?'*

Fanny nodded, dumbly, turning her eyes to the massive rocky pinnacle that seemed to glisten in the alpine air, piercing the clouds.

There was certainly something about a man in lederhosen . . . with a sudden creak, his lips were on hers, his muscular hands dexterously unlacing her Army and Navy Stores Hiking Dress. As the sunlight struck her navel, she gave a little gasp.

'Why,' she murmured into his sleek sunburnt cheek, 'I don't even know your name!'

'My name,' he panted, hastily ripping his lederhosen from their stanchions, 'is Hans Onneksperienz.'

'Mummee!' Harriet runs in. 'How often have you and Daddy sharpened a pencil?'

Mystified. Inform her that such a thing cannot be reckoned, and point out that we mostly use felt-tips these days. Then divine from her saucy expression that *sharpening a pencil* is a devilish infantile metaphor. Invite Harriet to guess, at which she ponders deeply and then suggests, 'Eight?' Recall what an aberration sex seemed to my childish fancy.

The interrogation continues. If the Daddies produce millions of seeds, why do the Mummies only have one or two babies? Suggest it is perhaps because one baby is enough to ensure complete prostration, which she takes as a personal insult, punches me and runs off.

Rest of day dedicated to detection and eradication of various household stinks. Divert myself mentally by casting the film-of-the-book *Beefy on Broadway* or *Botham in Gotham*. Botham to be played by Gerard Depardieu and Gooch by Sylvester Stallone, but am rather perplexed when it comes to Gower's girlish beauty. Joely Richardson in drag, perhaps.

Fall exhausted into bed at midnight, and discover, to my chagrin, that Spouse is intent on pencil-sharpening.

seventy-eight

AUGUSTUS: THE ROMAN MONTH. Reasons to be cheerful: first two weeks of school hols successfully concluded, without loss of sanity; Spouse's summer school now over, so he cannot any longer avoid his share of childcare; Mrs Body has gone off to Marbella for two weeks so no need to tidy up before she comes. Also Prime Minister says *bastard*. He should have said it months ago.

Henry camping with Julian so only Harriet to cope with. Not sure if this is a reason to be cheerful, actually. Shortage of little friends to play with means that I become an enormous little friend. (Over ten stone again and less than a month to the beaches of Gower.)

'You're the Queen and I'm the Princess and we're dressing up to go to the ball!'

Another reason to be cheerful: one is not the Queen. One spends one's childhood wishing one was, and then the rest of one's life thanking God one isn't one of the Royal ones.

Tiring of attiring, Harriet demands money. She has nearly saved up enough for a Polly Pocket clock. Of all the twee knick-knacks offered to little girls, the Polly Pocket stuff is the least offensive. Lilliputian people half an inch high live inside a small plastic case resembling a powder compact, where they enjoy a range of ingeniously contrived comforts: tiny kitchens with all mod cons, teensy swimming pools no bigger than a thimble . . . a bit like Japan, I suppose.

'I really need a clock! You said so yourself, Mummy, 'cos I wouldn't wake you up too early in the morning then.'

A deal is struck. She may have the Polly Pocket clock if she first cleans the car.

'Oh, ace! Can I have a bucket of water, Mummy, and a sponge and some of that car wash stuff and –'

Wonder why I ever suggested it, but doggedly set the whole débâcle in motion. At the first squirt my T-shirt is saturated so withdraw to the house. Halfway up the stairs I am summoned to the attic by a deep growl from Spouse. Find him seated in old armchair amidst cartons spewing out papers – the Domum archive.

'I'm reading your old love letters,' he grins. Flinch, expecting sardonic comment, but instead his eyes flicker lewdly over my wet T-shirt, he pulls me down upon his lap and kisses me rapaciously on the mouth, something that has not happened in daylight within living memory. After a brief resistance, I think, oh well, why not? The advantage of sex with somebody you've known for centuries is you can do it with your eyes shut. In fact, sometimes it's the only way you can do it.

'The wet T-shirt is a good idea,' he comments afterwards, 'but next time, leave the bra off.'

Too true. Laundry crisis owing to Mrs Body's holiday means I have been reduced to wearing my old maternity bras – effect akin to collapsed tents, in this case, soaked with rain.

Descend, adjusting clothing, and take Harriet in badly washed car to Woolworths. Behave foolishly on roundabout, but get away with it. Wonder how policeman would react to the excuse that I had just washed my car and couldn't do a thing with it.

In toy dept, discover that the knick-knackers have seized upon the Jurassic and one can now buy three-inch pink plastic dinosaurs with manes of peroxide hair and a comb: My Little Tyrannosaurus. Cannot think of a less suitable subject for tweeification, except perhaps My Little Merv, with huge moustache to comb.

Purchase Polly Pocket clock and Harriet, panting with lust, disembowels it in the back of the car on the way home.

'Oh it's lovely, Mummy, it's got Old Father Time in it!'

Congratulate myself on having bought a toy which refers, however glancingly, to cultural tradition, instead of being a perversion of nature.

'Help, Mummy! Old Father Time's gone down the back of the seat!'

'I can't stop the car now! Wait till we get home.'

Once home, lift up back seat to reveal congealed mass of old sweets, hairslides, parts of plastic monsters, but no Old Father Time. Perhaps he feared she might want to comb his beard.

'But I only had him for about five seconds!' wails Harriet. Tempted to observe that Time's a bit like that, but refrain.

seventy-nine

MRS BODY RETURNS FROM Marbella, disgusted with Abroad. Closer interrogation reveals that her disgust was provoked mainly by the behaviour of the British. Another reason for Euro-scepticism: it brings out the worst in us. Comfort her with brick-red tea and slices of Battenberg Cake. Is Battenberg named after some obscure European dynasty? If it was called Bradford-on-Avon Cake it would have been outlawed by EU edict by now.

Spouse enters, beams, admires Mrs Body's body (brick-red to match the tea), panders to her xenophobia, and then enquires if we may dump the kids on her on Sunday so we can go to the cricket – a foolish expedition, as he admits later, as English cricket has gone to the dogs.

Children readily acquiesce, as they will be able to ransack the Bodys' vile videos and perhaps devour oven chips shaped like dinosaur turds for tea. Weather is but so-so, but prospect of afternoon *à deux* beguiling: the crack of leather on willow, the flap of white flannel, etc. However, minutes before we are due to leave, Elaine rings to ask me over because she is a bit low. Invite her to cricket instead, at which she chirrups at the novelty of it all and runs off to dive into her sporty togs.

Sporty togs turn out to be glistening cream dress with pearls at throat and ears. Old men on the gate flirt with her, but I am apparently too old to ogle. Alice and Saskia would no doubt require me to be delighted thereat. Cannot help feeling a bit jealous instead, as own dress, and indeed own body, dowdy old tat. Cricketers, however, even worse dressed. No white flannel – instead horrid blue tracksuits.

'Supporting Gloucestershire,' announces Spouse, 'which used to be a pleasure, has now become social work.' Elaine breaks into a peal of merry laughter. I know Spouse is amusing occasionally, but he's not that funny. Still, he goes on, they're doing better now, and in the middle of the field she will see the best wicket-keeper in the world: Jack Russell.

'What!' cries Elaine. 'That little chap in the funny hat? He looks like one of the Flowerpot Men!' She giggles anew at the idea of his being a Jack Russell and says she is definitely a dog person. Evidently she is no longer a bit low. In fact I wonder if we will be able to get her home without her becoming entangled in a tree.

At about 3.30 a flickering halo of unearthly light hovers around Jack Russell's head. Is this a Sign from Heaven which Ted Dexter ignores at his peril? No, it is the first symptom of a migraine. Retire to tea-tent and take pills, in vain. Suddenly realise that Ted Dexter means Mr Right. Suppose this is one of God's little jokes.

Am driven home by Spouse with martyred air. Elaine sympathetic, though: soothes my throbbing brow with her wonderfully cool hand, and once home, puts me to bed, feeds the children, etc, despite my feeble insistence that Spouse can do it.

'Oh no, Dulcie, it's fine, I love it!' she whispers, her eyes alight with fun. 'It's horrible living alone, you've no idea!' More evidence perhaps of her being a dog person. Suspect I am a cat person, though rapidly inclining to the dodo. Left to my own thoughts in darkened room. Laughter below. *The Dog Star rages: say I'm sick, I'm dead.*

Brain as usual refuses to go and lie in its basket. Instead it gnaws away at the idea of dogs and cricket. Alan Border's Collies would top the Canine League. Can almost hear John Arlott growling, 'Their play has a mordant quality, a dogged perseverance . . .' Even their names sound like a pack of dogs barking. 'Mark! Mark! Waugh! Waugh! Warne! Warne! Warne! Boooooooooon!' Though Warne looks more like an engaging young pig who has had his snout in a bowl of cream. Drift off to sleep eventually, and dream of Edward de Bono and Ronnie Barker.

Awoken by Spouse coming to bed at half past midnight. 'Not tonight, dear, I've got a headache,' he quips, and falls instantly asleep. Next day worst pain has gone, but feel as if I am an old stone pillar that crashed down into undergrowth aeons ago.

'How are you, old thing?' enquires Spouse. Object to his endearment, and lament aloud that I am no longer as young as Elaine.

'She's a silly tart,' he snorts, and even though it is a transparent lie, am grateful. Such are the threadbare courtesies of middle-aged marriage.

Manoeuvre myself painfully into the kitchen to find – astonishing – a letter addressed to me in the handwriting of that frisky young dog, Tom the Plumber. Ah. Had forgot that old stone pillars can be of passing interest to frisky young dogs.

eighty

HELP! SHE'S NOT A bit like you. Badly in need of matrimonial counselling. Tom. What a cheek! One does not expect to have to dish out dry shoulders to one's ex-lovers. Scarcely a peep from him for months – since his wedding to the sturdy and scowling stone mason Sabrina. 'She's not a bit like you' – well, thank God for small mercies. That's the nearest to a compliment I've come to since Henry told me I was not too fat, really, except from the neck down.

Spouse comes in, and out of ancient habit I panic and slide Tom's card under the breadboard. It's strange how resiliently the guilt survives when the pleasure of extra-mural flings has become but a faded memory.

'What can we *do* today, Mummy?' wails Harriet, toying fretfully with her Pop-tart. 'The cornflakes have run out! And we're bored!'

'How can you sit there and say that?' I cry, 'when your toy cupboards are bursting with stuff, and and and when I was your age –' Speech judders to appropriately apoplectic halt.

Recall, before I had children, how I imagined I would cow them with deadly shafts of asperity. But now my deadly shafts have wilted into frayed old dish-mops of dither.

'Don't, erm – don't do that with your Pop-tart thing! Either eat it or – or well, eat it!'

'Have they got trampolines on the Gower?' enquires Henry, suspicious since I told him there were not, to my recollection, any swing-boats or video-games arcades but a dozen varieties of lovely seaweed including the crinkly forked *Chondrus*. 'Seaweeds collected for mounting on paper should be kept in water and carefully floated on to the surface of the immersed paper . . .' (*A Guide to Gower*, p. 100).

Henry refuses to show any interest in the idea of mounting seaweed, and Harriet shrieks at the idea of finding sponges called Dead Men's Fingers in the rockpools.

'We might find real dead men's fingers, though, mightn't we, Mummy?' Henry brightens at this thought. 'We might find a whole dead body in some undergrowth somewhere. We ought to get a dog, it would make it easier to find bodies.'

Remind children that Gower is not till the last week of the holidays, and till then they must confine themselves to finding dead bodies in the garden.

'And if they do,' ponders Spouse, also brightening, 'perhaps Helen Mirren will be round in her Detective role.'

Persuade him to take the children off to Berkeley Castle where they may imagine life in the good old days when royal disembowellings were not just metaphorical. He agrees on condition that it's My Turn Tomorrow.

Peace caused by their departure ruined by realisation that we have run out of loo paper. Nothing is worse than making this discovery whilst already fatally enthroned. Annoyed that I must waste some precious solitude driving to nearest SPAR (a Spar too Far for walking). Car has sudden fit of temper – emits angry buzzing when indicator switched on, and red warning light flashes suggesting battery trouble. Car also stops, though discover later this is only because I have taken my foot off the accelerator in panic at all the buzzing and flashing.

Manage, however, to acquire toilet roll, and arrive home looking forward to a couple of hours' tranquil bum-wiping and browsing in the wonderfully erudite Gower guidebook. 'The Rhinoceros and the Mammoth and even Aurignacian Man sheltered in Gower's caves.' But heart leaps instead to see familiar old van parked outside our house and a familiar tall figure, crowned with wild curls, ringing the doorbell.

Tom turns to me, revealing a vile beard, greets me with an ecstatic kiss, and we slither inside – furtively. Old habits die hard. Ransack cupboard in vain – have run out of tea. Offer him camomile, which he assures me he prefers. (I ask you, can this be a Man?)

'The thing is, Dulcie, she's so – I mean – well, there doesn't seem to be a spark between us any more.'

Think it perhaps wiser not to mention that I'm having the same trouble with my car. Also forbear to suggest that marrying somebody within a couple of months of meeting them might rather be asking for it.

'It's totally, like, well, like the Ice Age, yeah?' he moans, running his fingers through his hair in a feverish appeal for sympathy.

Just hope we haven't run out of that, as well.

eighty-one

MIXED FEELINGS SINCE TOM told me his marriage had come to resemble the Ice Age – in less than six months. Try hard to conjure up dismay, but am stalked instead by a sneaking triumph. Easier to sympathise with his difficulties in finding himself stepfather to two great lads taller than himself. Not so much stepfather as stepladderfather. Luckily Spouse and children returned from Berkeley Castle before Tom had time to get too soulful and doggy.

He did tell me, however, of glorious WOMAD day of world music in Bath on Sunday. Decide to take Henry and Harriet though Spouse excuses himself, preferring to bask in the TV's fluorescent flicker rather than be enchanted by joyous African drumming. Spouse would do anything to avoid being enchanted, especially by something Tom had recommended.

However, my heart skips as I drive west towards Bath – a happy place. Inform children this is where I realised I was pregnant with Henry.

'How did you know you were pregnant?' demands Harriet.

Realise, with a lurch, that this is the moment to spill the beans.

'Well, you know, the mother has a bean – I mean, a seed – ready to make into a baby?'

'Yeah?'

Suddenly turn left down a very narrow lane, for no good reason.

'Well, she makes lots and lots of seeds – one a month – and everything gets ready for the baby, and then if the daddy's seed doesn't come along, the seed, er, sort of goes off . . .'

'Goes bad? Ugh! Gross!'

'Well, not exactly –'

Getting very hot. Car appears around corner. Reverse for 200 yards between high hedges towards passing place.

'Not goes bad . . . just – oh crikey! – just – has to be discarded – has to go –'

'What was it I asked you?' muses Harriet.

'You asked how I knew I was pregnant.' Car passes me with half an inch to spare. Driver glares at me as if narrowness of lane is my fault.

'Can we have crisps?'

'No! I'm trying – trying to – anyway the old seed that's not any good any more comes out with a bit of blood and stuff. Oh, you bastard!' Lorry has appeared round corner.

'Blood!' Henry's ears prick up. 'Comes out of where?'

'Out of . . . ' Reversing again. 'Out of the mummy's baby-hole – just behind the pee place.'

'She means the vagina,' Harriet informs him. 'Does it hurt, Mummy?'

'Oh no!' Back of car enters hedge. Engine stalls. Lorry driver, up ahead, smiles in patronising manner. 'Not really. Hardly ever. It's just a little bit of blood . . . every month . . . called a period.'

'Have you ever had one?'

'Of course I have ! Every month!'

'There's no need to shout at me, Mummy! I didn't *know*!'

'Sorry . . . sorry . . . it's a pleasure, you swine.' Lorry passes me with pitying leer. Start off up lane again. Lane appears to be shrinking. Wonder if I am re-enacting birth. Will need forceps to get us out. Just as I am thinking this, giant pair of motorised forceps appears up ahead. Some agricultural vehicle. Reverse back to main road, still engrossed in the cyclical mysteries.

'But you still haven't told us how you knew you were pregnant!'

'Ah! Oh! Yes! Sod it!'

'Don't *swear*! You tell us not to!'

'No. Right. Of course. Well, you know the seed's going to grow into a baby if it doesn't come out with blood and stuff.'

'I would have thought,' muses Harriet, 'that you could tell you were pregnant because your tummy got all big.'

There is a long silence. I decide to surrender to the inevitable, reverse right back into the main road and vow never to leave it again.

'If anyone wants to know how to kill a dog,' observes Henry considerately, 'you pull its legs apart.'

The conversation thus redirected along the paths of decorum, we drive serenely on. But Bath turns out to be entirely empty of African music. Tom must have got the wrong day. Mustn't tell Spouse. And anyway, just being there felt like a triumph after so many reverses.

eighty-two

ON THE EVE OF our departure for Gower, news of a sensational hammer murder disgusts the nation. Ask Spouse whether he would ever dream of killing his family with a hammer but instead of providing the expected reply ('often'), he feels his armpits, looks pale and says he feels giddy.

'Oh, *don't* say you're going down with a bug!' I howl. But so it proves. Spouse takes to his bed and begs us to go on and leave him behind, in the great tradition of British explorers. Bite lip, pack up entire household, carry sixteen loads of heavy stuff to sledge, and marshal huskies.

'I'll come as soon as I'm fit,' he groans. 'Sorry darling.' Darling be damned. Spare me that.

Extensive roadworks on M4 turn Spouse's Estimated Journey Time (one and a half hours from Severn Bridge) into four hours of boiling inertia.

'Oh, *how* much *longer*?' screams Harriet in agony. 'You *said* it wouldn't be long!'

'I thought it wouldn't be *long*!'

'Well *how* much *longer*?'

'I don't know! It depends on the traffic! Stop yelling at me!'

'You're the one who's *yelling*, Mummy! This is the *worst* day of my *life*!'

Harriet bursts into hysterical sobs and Henry seizes his chance.

'Can I have a snorkel mask, Mum? For being good?'

Don't know which is worse – her being bad or him being good.

Eventually arrive at beautiful bay surrounded by wooded hills. Collect key and locate cottage down remote lane. Idyllic, but it takes five minutes to open door following landlady's instructions to jiggle it about a bit. When the back door finally yields to our jiggling we are catapulted into tiny but supernaturally clean kitchen. The sight of a mop and bucket reinforces my instinct that this holiday is to be a far-from-Cipriani experience.

Burglar alarm beeps at our entry, but landlady has forewarned me and I stride competently to silence it. Enjoy the moment as this is the last competent striding I shall do for some time.

Stagger blaspheming to and from car, unloading effluvia of civilisation. Beg children to help, but they are distracted by horses looking over our garden wall. Within three minutes all my carefully packed organic carrots and apples have disappeared down their throats. Harriet runs up wearing an expression of equine ecstasy.

'Oh, Mummy, aren't they sweet! I've called them Lightning and Star!' Inform her sternly that the most rare and interesting animal hereabouts is a microscopic snail called Vertigo, at which she cries *Oh gross!* and runs away.

Cook chicken, causing smoke detector to shriek; hot water mysteriously runs out after one and a half inches, causing children to shriek; kitchen door jams, marooning me within – exit effected only with assistance of breadknife. Wonder if I packed enough shrieks. Feel wave of homesick nostalgia for hot water and doors you can walk through, but bravely tell children holiday will be brilliant just wait and see. Soon they are asleep in twin-bedded room with cot ('Oh, what a waste, Mummy! You should've had another baby!').

I take an early bath. Leave door open the better to hear intruders breaking in downstairs. Maniac with hammer. Or Grim Reaper with sickle. At the sound of heavy breathing I freeze in my tepid two inches – but it is only Henry on nasal manoeuvres. As I slip into my nightie, I hear a stealthy rubbing and whickering outside in garden. Evidently the intruder preparing to penetrate.

Decide to sleep with children so I can gallantly fight for their lives with Squeegee mop – only weapon available. (Breadknife too bloody – would prefer vegetarian murder.) Transfer the sleeping Harriet to cot. Then discover that, by taking all the drawers out of the chest and laying them end-to-end on the floor, I can barricade door. Go downstairs for bucket in case I need to pee in my nocturnal stronghold. Wonder if mop and bucket will be effective defence against hammer and sickle. Oh well. At least it's irreproachably proletarian.

Drift off into an uneasy sleep, knowing that when this relaxing idyll is over, I must return to Rusbridge and gird up my loins for Aunt Elspeth.

eighty-three

GREAT AUNT ELSPETH COCKS an alert ear. 'Ah, listen, dearr! The robin is singing his autumn song!' Have always thought this was rather tactless of the robin. Harriet's fluorescent green plastic frisbee is also singing its autumn song. Free with Rice Krispies, it destroys my brain with a series of blood-curdling electronic shrieks as it flies about.

'Autumn is such a wonderful season! So brrracing!' Cannot agree. Detest sinking, rotting, darkening feeling. However, grateful for excuse to veil my corporeal corpulence in loose, enveloping clothes. But Aunt Elspeth's birthday present to me goes too far. She has knitted me a vast oatmeal-coloured sack into which I struggle, a smile of intense delight heroically nailed to my face.

'It's a tunic, dearr! They're all the rage, these days, aren't they?' Forbear to mention that colourless colours such as oatmeal make me look ill and fat. At this unpropitious moment Spouse enters and his aunt begs him to admit how ravishing I look in her sack. Spouse assures her that it gives me the tempting radiance of a sago pudding.

Aunt E. volunteers to babysit so Spouse can take me out for a candlelit dinner *à deux* – to complete the seductive business started by the oatmeal sack. We assure her that we cannot contemplate an outing without her, and by some curious planetary conjunction we manage to invite Bernard and Audrey Twill next door as well. Tracey Body is to babysit, and we are to dine at Rusbridge's new Thai restaurant, the Phuket Beach.

It is pronounced Poo-quette, I sternly inform the children. 'It sounds like something you wipe your bum with!' cries Harriet. 'Like a serviette for the other end!' Recall Jilly Cooper's warning that serviette is an irredeemably vulgar word, but it arrived with Aunt Elspeth, along with doilies, toilet and pardon. Also recall Jilly Cooper's child announcing that Mummy Says Pardon is much worse word that Phuket.

Aunt Elspeth and the Twills plainly queasy at the thought of foreign food, but Spouse assures them they are much more likely to get food poisoning here at 196 Cranford Gardens. Try not to feel too insulted at this remark, though aware that less than an hour ago I found a saucepan full of pre-war soup in the fridge and tipped it down the loo, averting my gaze as the bits of mould fizzed and frothed.

Audrey Twill is driven to conjure up a sick-headache to escape, though we all suspect she is secretly gobbling Spam sandwiches and watching *Keeping up Appearances* whilst we get to grips with the Orient. Unlike the sonorous gongs, twangs and clucks of Chinese, Thai seems to be a language which has been chopped fiercely into four-letter words. Aunt Elspeth peruses the menu with maidenly hesitation.

'I can't decide between *Prat Suk Tank* and *Honk Wak Prik*,' she ponders. Bernard Twill, thwarted in his search for a steak on the menu, settles for *Duk Phuk Konk* with a fatalistic sigh that shows he fears it may lead to *Sik Kum Kwik*. Spouse orders melodiously: 24, 32, 18, 37, 47 and a pot of Thai tea.

The food is exquisitely prepared and presented, and garnished with a turnip carved in the shape of a rosebud. Somehow this reminds me of how I always feel when I dress up to go out to parties. Aunt Elspeth enquires whether Thailand used to be Siam but assumes it has gone the way of Persia, Montgomery-shire, Bletchley, and other poetic delights.

Bernard Twill decides to try Thai beer (*Won Suk Nok Bak Phlat Out On Phlor*) and under its influence becomes gallant, a ghastly sight. He informs Aunt Elspeth that he has always wanted to be a toyboy but he has missed the boat, born too early, dammit, unless of course she is willing to recruit him.

Aunt Elspeth clearly deeply offended by his assumption that he is younger than her, even though it is obvious to all concerned. I attempt to distract with a paean of praise for maturity, and lie that Spouse has become infinitely more attractive to me since he started to go thin on top. Spouse glares at me. Aunt Elspeth glares at Bernard. The Thai tea goes cold.

'Well, you should know, Dulcie!' cries Bernard in a desperate attempt to dredge up the conversation. 'You're the expert where toyboys are concerned, hey? Hey? Haw, haw!'

'What on earrth do you mean?' enquires Aunt Elspeth, turning upon the hapless Twill her iciest stare. This is clearly the moment to Thai die, but just as I am about to close my eyes, Spouse dextrously tips the remains of the *Duk Phuk Konk* into Aunt Elspeth's tweed lap. God, how I love that man.

eighty-four

We deliver Bernard Twill home, replete with Thai food and enchanted with Great Aunt Elspeth.

'You must take one of my marrows back to Scotland with you, Mrs MacIvor!' he insists, hesitating by his gate.

'I'm sorry,' snaps Aunt E., 'but marrows bring on my diverticulitis. I would be rrretching all night.' Aunt can deter the most persistent suitor with one martial roll of her Rs. And she took against the inoffensive Twill for some reason, even though he once had a dog called Hamish that looked for all the world like a sporran on legs.

We are welcomed by Tracey Body, babysitter, a splendid sight this autumn. A crew-cut, a sloppy joe down to the fingertips, chain mail leggings, donkey jacket and stern Doc Marten boots complete her ensemble. Admire the current girls-as-navvies syndrome. Secretly attracted to the idea of Doc Marten boots as they look so rugged and comfy, but fear I might present a ludicrous spectacle therein: mutton dressed as ram.

Tracey reports that all is well though Harriet was in floods of tears earlier as her fluorescent green frisbee whizzed up the garden and landed atop a steep inaccessible bank covered with nettles. Evidently the chain mail and tough boots are merely cosmetic. Tracey is a sheep in wolf's clothing.

Sheepishly discover I have no money with which to pay her, but am rescued by Aunt Elspeth. She doles out the ready, however, with pursed lips and pursed purse and as soon as Tracey has gone, informs me that I pay that gairrl far too much. Agree heartily, which takes the wind out of Great Aunt's sails. But only for a split second.

'What on earrth was that Twill man saying about you and toyboys, Dulcie?'

'Oh, I had a lodger whilst Gordon was in America.' Was preparing this all the way home, as I know that Elspeth, like squirrel, always remembers where the juiciest nuts have been buried. 'A young chap. Plumber. As wet as a weekend in Manchester.'

'And Dulcie had a mad passionate affair with him,' grins Spouse, looking up from the obituary column. I blush and Elspeth bridles.

'Gordon! Don't insult poorr Dulcie! She has more taste than to behave like that! Toyboys indeed!' And Aunt Elspeth marched upstairs to divest herself of the tweed skirt, marred by Thai cuisine. This leaves myself and Spouse suddenly and self-consciously alone.

'It's rather ironical, isn't it?' says Spouse with a strange *louche* air. Panic flaps in my throat like mad hen in sack.

'What is?'

'Him being so wet. And a plumber.'

Produce enormous stage groan, and hasten to put kettle on, necessitating turning my back on Spouse for precious ten seconds.

'He wasn't so bad really,' I sigh, as if recalling tiresome mediocrity. 'He just needed mothering. He was going through a very –'

'Oh, spare me all that.' Spouse yawns. 'I can't stand blokes who go through things. Get me a glass of whisky, will you? I'm too lazy to move.'

Oblige, with mixed motives. Spouse finds sports page and sinks into it like large stone into deep well. He should set up Anti-Counselling Service, sponsored by Monday Club. Get on yer bike. Pull yerself together. Car stolen? Well bloody walk, you idle git. Never did me any harm. Dying of hypothermia? Knit yerself a woolly hat. Feeling sorry for yourself? Take that you bastard, etc. He could be the Man from the Min of Agg.

Wonder if Spouse's truculent verbal artillery hides a tender, palpitating heart. Is he, like Tracey, lamb dressed as Rambo? Think not. However tender Spouse's heart may originally have been, it must be bulletproof now after marinating for over forty years in the habitual vinegar of his sensibility.

What is he thinking? No idea. Kettle boils. Make tea. Lapsang Souchong. Nice name for a girl. Bring out the cheese and biscuits. That's the thing about eastern food: hungry again half an hour later. Rather like adultery, as I dimly recall.

'Thanks,' says Spouse, wolfing down huge lump of cheese, hugging my hip and reading the sports page. 'You're not a bad old stick. If I was a toyboy I'd fancy you myself.'

Next day, sting myself in sixteen places rescuing the frisbee. Oh well. Only fair. Dame Nature's revenge. She knows, y'know.

eighty-five

INVITED TO MRS BODY'S son's wedding. Mrs Body informs us it is to be a proper church wedding with all the trimmings. Feel obscurely guilty that Spouse and I got spliced at Register Office even though at the time it seemed wonderfully rational and sane. Exchanged secret alternative vows, too. Recall lying in punt under willows, whilst Spouse-to-be stared into my eyes through enormously long hair (his) and murmured romantically, 'I don't own you. You don't own me. Jealousy is a barbaric emotion. Beneath contempt.' Shelley would've been proud of us.

But Harriet isn't. She searches in vain through my wardrobe for white satin and lace of my old wedding dress. Cannot face telling her it was a grey crêpe Ossie Clark number that rotted right through at the armpits shortly afterwards, probably due to strenuous avoidance of jealousy. I inform her, however, that she can wear her beautiful blue satin frilly dress, at last. But Harriet sighs.

'I think I've got past that stage, Mummy,' she confides. 'What I really want to wear is black leggings, black T-shirt and vampire fangs.' Spouse outraged to discover he has grown too stout for his suit. Aunt Elspeth, on the point of returning to Kirkwhinnie, advises him to try charity shops as they are a wonderrful rrresourrce. This appeals to Spouse's frugality, and at Rusbridge Oxfam shop he is suitably suited with a grey pinstripe. A snip at £4.50. Costs twice that amount to have it dry-cleaned.

Eventually great day dawns. Bride is a country girl so we drive out to ancient Church of St John in the remote Wiltshire village of Little Sodding. St John's evidently thriving, though comforting to know that if not, it would be cared for by the Redundant Churches Fund. Seem to recall HQ used to be at St Andrew-by-the-Wardrobe, in London. What was St Andrew doing by the wardrobe? Sounds more furtive than saintly.

Wonder if one day there will be a Redundant Wives Fund, and if so, who will be its Royal Patroness.

Arrive early and read pamphlet. 'St John's is remarkable for the outstanding corbels and gargoyles, some representing devils and some local people.' Gaze upwards but cannot spot the difference. Rick neck. Harriet sulks in her satin. Henry fiddles with small plastic replica of killing machine. Spouse dozes in his Oxfam pinstripe.

Weep copiously during ceremony, much to Harriet's indignation. The idealistic impulse always reduces me to tears. Complete lack of tissues and hankies requires me to snivel into the only absorbent thing in my handbag: a five-pound note. What you might call a run on the pound.

At the reception afterwards, I find myself next to Tracey Body who has acknowledged the solemnity of the occasion by having a sparkling stone inserted into her nose. I enquire of her who is that handsome girl talking to her Mum.

'That's my cousin Debra.'

Ask if the middle-aged woman behind her is Debra's mother as they are so alike. (Nose like Concorde.) Tracey confirms this *aperçu*. Enquire which gent is Debra's father. Tracey informs me nobody knows who is Debra's father nor Pauline's neither. Is Pauline Debra's sister, then, I wonder?

'No, Pauline's Mum's our Auntie Angie, and Debra's is Auntie Joan, look.'

Admire handsome youth ('Our Darren' – another cousin) and ask if his parentage has been established.

'Oh, yeah, his Dad was our Uncle Bob, only he done a runner like when Darren was five and nobody ent seen 'im since.' Am fascinated by this social history, and appalled to find that despite our anti-matrimonial vows of long ago, Spouse and I appear to be the nearest thing, at this wedding, to a respectable old married couple. Feel a deep sense of failure.

Mrs Body, resplendent in rippling polyester pleats, accepts my congratulations on the handsomeness of her son, the evident good fortune of the bride, etc. But Spouse cannot resist boasting about how he got his suit for £4.50 from the Oxfam shop. Mrs Body congratulates him, but I can tell she is hurt that he did not shell out real money in her son's honour. Give Spouse a dirty look, but he only beams in a way which suggests too much alcohol has wrought that occasional Darwinian miracle: he has evolved for an hour or so into a warm-blooded animal.

Return home exhausted to find a card on doormat with bleak message in Tom's hectic italic: *My marriage is over.*

eighty-six

'LET'S HOPE HIS PLUMBING lasts longer than his relationships,' observes Spouse. Still think fondly of Tom every time I use the bidet. Not sure whether I should be dismayed at his news or secretly triumphant. Decide on triumph. If life follows usual course, there will be plenty of opportunity for dismay later in the day.

Coincidentally, Elaine-across-the-road rings asking to be reminded of Tom's telephone number as her sink is blocked. Reluctantly oblige. Still fear lest Tom and Elaine should become enamoured and want to shed their horrible glow over me.

'You don't need a plumber to unblock a bloody sink,' sneers Spouse. 'Ring the silly tart back and tell her I'll come and sort it out in five minutes.'

Grateful for this chance to thwart the designs of Eros. Moreover, sink-unblocker a v. suitable role for Spouse – he is so caustic, all he would need to do is flush himself down the plughole.

Buy gammon joint for Sunday lunch, and *Beauty and the Beast* video for Harriet who has earned it by clearing-out-and-throwing-away activities on unprecedented scale over past week. Rather like Labour Party Conference. Henry also made pretence at tidying his bedroom but one glance informed me that all his garbage was hidden away under the bed. Rather like Conservative Party Conference. Drive home deafened by children's back-seat arguments and fantasise miserably about how I could silence them with one flash of my teeth if I had any clout. Rather like Liberal Party Conference.

Arrive home and immerse gammon in cold water to soak overnight. At least I can assert myself over things that are dead.

Sunday morning. Discover Spouse asked Elaine over to lunch when he fixed her sink. Pleased that he managed a social impulse, but express the hope that the children will not be too awful. Spouse reminds me that Elaine seems to like children being awful. Noise and misbehaviour a wholesome organic alternative to the sterile elegance of her empty life, I suppose. Although grateful that my life is full, wish it would not, like vacuum cleaner bag, burst all over the carpet quite so often.

'Mummee! Can we have mint sauce?' shrieks Harriet. Not with ham I insist. Why not, she demands. Wonder for a moment if I am being a reactionary old fart. Why not mint sauce with ham, indeed with bread pudding or Bakewell tart? Why not a dab of mint sauce behind each ear? (Glutton dressed as lamb.) (Why obsessed with mutton recently?)

Mint sauce relatively easy to make, unlike the dreaded parsley variety. Aware that I shall shortly have to wrestle with flour, butter and milk on a relentless voyage towards green-flecked wallpaper paste.

Elaine, bless her, eats heartily and is the life and soul of the Sunday lunch. She has brought a catalogue of stocking fillers for the children to peruse.

'Look, Mum!' shouts Henry. 'Everything you need to be a spy for only £2.99!'

A spin-off, presumably, of the de-mystification of MI5.

After lunch we are implored by Harriet to watch *Beauty and the Beast*. Wonderful until the 'happy ending' where the lumbering but lovable Beast turns into disastrously naff Prince. This, of course, is what they're trying to do to the Labour Party. Speaking of which, Gordon Brown really must stop trying to smile. His token grins are an irritating interruption of his habitual sombre grandeur. He and Peter Sissons are brothers in *gravitas*. Sombreros.

Express the oft-felt disappointment that there are only three main parties to vote for. Oh yes, sighs Spouse, and only two sexes – what a bore. Rather surprised at this remark. Had thought that even two sexes were too much of a challenge for Spouse. He would be much happier as a herbaceous perennial, leaving it to the bees to distribute his genetic material without the necessity for conversation, and dropping into a deep sleep from October to April.

If Spouse were a plant he would be Monkshood: tall, dark and poisonous. Elaine would be svelte and elegant Snake's Head Fritillary. Children would be Ground Elder. Tom . . .

Tom would be rampant and romping Russian Vine, and I would be rotten old shed, groaning under his advances. Must remember that, no matter how delightfully post-matrimonial he may have become.

eighty-seven

ALICE AND SASKIA ARRIVE for the weekend. Their relationship has evidently blossomed anew after Alice's disenchantment with the fickle Elly. Saskia has gone back to teaching as times are hard and there is little demand, these days, for her wall-mounted collages of wooden spoons, frying pans and fragments of apron ('Monuments to Domestic Enslavement, 10,000 BC to 1993', The Old Bakehouse Gallery, Throckston Gullet – where it bombed.)

'Honestly, going back to teaching is like being thrown to the lions,' she groans, warming herself piteously around a cup of elderflower tea. Agree that children can be absolute swine, whereat Harriet and Henry rise up sizzling indignantly from their pizzas, and Saskia cries, 'No, Dulcie – it's not the kids, it's the curriculum. Drama is on the way out, you know. Technology is squeezing everything else off the timetable.'

'What? No Drama?' Horrified to hear this, as Drama was the only lesson I enjoyed at Sir Steven Norris's Grammar School for Girls. Mind you, all we ever did was read *King Lear* aloud. The casting was a disgrace, too. Wendy Ashton got the part of Lear, even though I was the only bearded baritone in the Lower Sixth.

'It's the new Puritanism,' thunders Spouse unexpectedly, putting down his paper and glaring at us all as if it's our fault. 'Prudes to right of us, prudes to left of us. I don't know which is worse, family values or political correctness. Do they think, because they are virtuous, there shall be no more cakes and ale?'

'And ginger shall be hot in the mouth!' cries Alice. 'Amen!'

'Mummy,' Harriet whispers, 'who is Ginger? And what's a prude?'

'But, Mummy!' shouts Henry, 'I like Technology!'

The phone rings. The doorbell rings. Technology can speak for itself.

I grab the phone, assuming it will offer the longer distraction. Spouse heads for the hall. Alice and Saskia, as usual, have brought a whirlwind of polemic to our table and fostered between Spouse and myself a secret *entente*: the solidarity of the knackered. And now the voice of Tom buzzes in my ear: Tom, whose marriage is collapsing. Allegedly.

'Hi, Dulcie. I'm just round the corner: can we talk?'

'Well . . . it's a bit . . . we've got some friends staying . . .'

Spouse comes back in and introduces the newly-arrived Elaine to Alice and Saskia, who visibly bridle at her high heels.

'Oh shit!' says the phone, rather unpleasantly. 'I was hoping I might be able to crash out on your floor.'

'What!? Has she actually thrown you out?'

At this ejaculation the company falls silent and eavesdrops except for Harriet who yells, 'Who is it, Mummy?'

'Never mind,' Tom sulks Telecomically. 'I'll push off then –'

'Oh, Tom! Don't be like that! We can't put you up at the moment but at least come round for a cuppa and tell us all the gory details!'

'He can stay at my place!' trills Elaine, ever eager for diversion. My heart sinks, and I suffer acute pangs of dog-in-the-manger.

'Elaine says you can stay at her place.'

'What? Terrific! Tell her she's an angel. I'll be right over.'

Replace phone, and inform Elaine she is extra-terrestrial.

'Is this the Prodigal, er – Tom?' asks Alice, slipping into tact at the last moment. 'How very intriguing. I haven't seen him since, er.'

Wonder how many people in the room knew that Tom and I enjoyed a frenzied love affair for almost two years. One thing certain: those who do know are speculating feverishly about who else knows. Put on kettle as feel that fortifications may be necessary. The sun comes out, for the first time this autumn, and veils my head in warmth. Is this a sign?

'You're not dyeing your hair, are you, Dulcie?' asks Alice, following some rogue train of thought about toyboys, perhaps. 'You know what Germaine says. Love your grey.' Turning to give Harriet a warning glance, I bash the teapot against the tap and knock its spout off.

'Well done, Dulcie,' beams Saskia. 'Of all the domestic artefacts, teapots embody the most ludicrous phallocentricity.'

'Ah well,' grins Spouse. 'With all that Technology on the curriculum, our kids will be able to design their own, based on the famous accuracy with which women wee.' Oh God. Now he's done it. Alice scowls: kettle boils: doorbell rings: Tom looms. A few more of my hairs turn grey, with audible twang. 'On the other hand,' Spouse continues, 'you'd think the Government would realise that Drama is the best preparation for life there is.' As usual, Spouse speaketh more truth than he knoweth.

eighty-eight

ENTER TOM, STAGE LEFT, matrimonially semi-detached. Henry and Harriet rush to embrace him: Alice, Saskia and

Elaine beam in anticipation of juicy details: Spouse bestows welcoming sneer: I drop a cup on my foot.

'Hi, guys!' cries Tom, triumphant in disaster, looking at everybody except me. Does this mean he is still a tad in love with me? And what is a tad anyway? It has an amphibious sound. I fear it is a Transatlantic import, like a zit. 'I brought ya a pumpkin!'

The children fall on the pumpkin bellowing like hounds: *I want to do it. No, me! Mummy, he elbowed me*, etc. In tradition of British foreign policy, I award knives to the combatants and request a seemly carve-up.

'Tom!' cries Elaine avidly, 'I hear you're homeless. Has Sabrina chucked you out?'

'No, I left,' insists Tom with dignity.

'You poor thing!' purrs Elaine. 'Come and tell us all about it.' She pats the chair next to her, and Tom obliges, smiling foolishly into her rather unnecessarily large and lustrous eyes. No, he is not even a zit still in love with me.

'Tea? Coffee? Elderflower?' I enquire. 'Camomile? Rosehip?'

'Brandy?' asks Spouse.

'Diet Pepsi?' howls Harriet, desperate to dispense with her few remaining teeth. Tom goes for camomile, at which Spouse's sneer deepens. Tempted for a split second to shout *Wipe that grin off your face – his is bigger than yours if you really must know!* – but heroically refrain.

'So what's Sabrina done to deserve this?' asks Alice sternly.

'It's not what she's done,' says Tom. 'It's what she is. She sucks my blood. She's a vampire.' Observe that, as a vegetarian, Tom must find this particularly distressing. He does not laugh. This is serious stuff. 'She wants to suck all the life out of me. *Where have you been, who did you talk to, you're ten minutes late, what the hell's going on?*'

'Mummy! I want to be a vampire!' cries Harriet and runs out of the room. Henry chases her. Saskia, who has been watching the children with envy, grabs the vacated pumpkin and stabs. Tom resumes his lament.

'Also she's got these two great louts who abuse her with impunity. I say, "Don't talk to your Mum like that", and they say, "Shut it four-eyes". And then she says, "Leave them alone". Family life? You can keep it.'

'Right!' beams Alice. 'The family is a tomb for the living.'

Wonder if this is so, why she willingly entombs herself *chez nous* so often. Observe that Saskia's pumpkin has begun its inevitable journey towards Norman Lamont. How very *démodé* to have Yesterday's Pumpkin.

'How can you say that?' demands Elaine. 'I think families are lovely. Whenever I come over here, it's all noisy and friendly and cosy and – well, I wish I was part of a family.'

Children rush in with deafening invitation to smell Harriet's finger. Decline, and administer warning look, in vain.

'Oh, for God's sake!' screams Alice. 'How I loathe hearing a woman saying she wishes she had a family! Slavery! Is that what you want?'

'Not at all!' Elaine is getting steamed up, unlike Alice, whose anger is merely something she pulls on like an extra sweater. 'What's wrong with being loved? And wanting someone to love?'

Spouse gets up, as usual when love is mentioned, and walks out of the room, saying we must excuse him as he wants to watch football in the catacomb. Elaine gazes sentimentally at Harriet, who has climbed on to my knee. Suddenly, with treacherous thrust, Harriet sticks her finger up my nose. Moment of horror. Shriek. Children roll around roaring with laughter.

'Harriet stuck it up her bum, Mum!'

'That was vile, Harriet! Go and wash your hands!'

'Why can't you live for yourself?' Alice persists. 'Books, travel, friends, interesting work, ideas, politics, campaigns – you're young, fit and healthy – what more do you want?'

'I like the idea of caring,' says Elaine. 'Caring for others.'

'Sounds like Virginia Bottomley,' shudders Alice.

The children exult at the wonder of this name. Henry gasps: 'She's stuck her finger up her – Virginia Bottomley!'

Fight off revelation that this is exactly what the Honourable Lady needs.

'Well, anyway,' remarks Saskia, finishing off Norman Lamont's teeth, 'you can care for Tom now. You could make your place a hostel for battered husbands.' Elaine's eyes light up in a way which suggests that we may be watching history in the making.

eighty-nine

TOM IS ACCOMMODATED IN Elaine's spare room (or so we trust) for the duration of his matrimonial hostilities. They (this word, hitherto harmless, has acquired an unpleasant stink) announce that *they* are having a bonfire party. Something childish in the giving of parties together in their situation. Like playing Mummies and Daddies. All the same, grateful that this means we won't have to do anything, not even drive the kids to St Norman's College Playing Fields where Rusbridge stages its annual display in aid of charity, and at which event my fears of the dark, crowds, open spaces and fire all collide in a spectacular attack of quadraphobia.

Besides, Elaine has a way with a sausage. She is also, Tom proudly informs us, to attempt parkin. Never quite sure what parkin is, apart from the best female Prime Minister we never had – yet, anyway. Distraught by the ghostly persistence of Tory Government long after the pulse has failed. Amusing how they bang on about democracy all the time. As if we invented it . . . as if we actually *experienced* it, nowadays.

Feel a fleeting pang of regret that I am not up to organising a Green Coup. Would quite like creeping about under the Houses of Parliament with pots and pots of Russian Vine. Or would it be easier to penetrate what has become, under John Major, Drowning Street? (As in Not Waving but Drowning.) Refuse to think about Tom, despite the recurrence in my metaphorical artillery of Russian Vine.

Harriet rushes in and coughs all over me crying, 'It's croup, Mummy! I've got it off Ben Whitehead! And I think I love him! But Mr Lamb won't let me sit next to him any more! I have to sit next to Jasmine and she smells!' Rub Harriet's chest absently, lamenting my inability to organise croup, let alone coup. Suggest that if she has croup she it too ill for the fireworks, at which she explodes, filling the air with sulphurous language, and soars off crackling into the ionosphere.

'I think I'm getting too old for fireworks,' announces Spouse, who has been anti-inflammatory since he was twelve.

Wrap whole family in Vick and wool, though Bacofoil might be more appropriate, and cross road to Elaine's. Car hurtles past at 60 m.p.h., full of teenagers.

'I suppose it's only a matter of time before the Volvo gets nicked by joyriders,' I sigh.

'Nobody,' Spouse informs me with deepest disdain, 'would ever be tempted to steal that old heap.'

Deeply hurt by Spouse's frequent attempts to consign my dear old car to the junkyard – or in its case, Volholla. Dare not tell him it has started speaking to me. Only last week it whispered '*Hello Dolcie Poll mij hondbrok*' in a voice not unlike Max von Sydow's.

Welcomed by Elaine, unpleasantly elated – one assumes by presence of Tom. Amazed by vast bonfire presided over by most realistic and handsome guy I have ever seen. Seems a shame to burn him: I stroke his feet admiringly, at which he slowly keels over on to my head. This is the nearest I have come recently to a meaningful relationship with a member of the opposite sex. Perhaps this is why I am in danger of falling in love with my car.

Children delighted by bangers and bangers. Tom lets off rockets with perfect timing: Spouse placated with hot alcoholic toddy. Obscurely annoyed by the excellence of the whole event. My own guys, in the past, have been little better than dolls. Not that dolls are inferior to guys. Heck, no. They've just got to learn to believe in themselves.

'Met an admirer of yours the other day,' says Tom, a remark which for some reason I find particularly tasteless. 'Harriet's teacher. I sorted his bath out for him. He said you'd recommended me.'

'What, the wally with the earring and the cricket sweater?' sneers Spouse. 'What's his name? Sebastian Sheep?'

'Christopher Lamb,' I inform him. 'And I thought the cricket sweater was rather fetching. Lamb dressed as Hutton.'

'Well, he certainly fancies you, Dulcie.' Wish Tom wouldn't try to divert me from memories of our fling by kindling a dalliance for me with Harriet's teacher. 'He says you've got wonderfully hairy legs, and the face of a Polish countess.' Attempt to ignore this, but am sneakingly intrigued. 'Just thought I'd light the blue touch paper,' grins Tom, retiring immediately towards Elaine's delicious parkin.

'It's well known,' comments Spouse, 'that Polish countesses all look like the late lamented Les Dawson.'

ninety

SPOUSE AWAY AT A meeting, something to do with history. I think some of his fellow shitorians, as he calls them, are worried that History, like Drama, may be in danger of being shouldered out of the educational nest by the cuckoo Technology. A sort of Historectomy. To avoid this, there is a gathering of Past Masters – and Past Mistresses, too, I expect. In Brighton.

Irritated that weekend's childcare will be mine, all mine, when what I really need is a few hours' solitude to crank up my flagging Bonkbuster. (Recent enquiry from patient publisher reminded me that my heroine, Fanny, is marooned somewhere south of the Alps, and that more Eurotrash is required from my pen ere Christmas.) Why don't romantic novelists hold conference in Brighton leaving Spouses to juggle the roast potatoes? Unlike history, escapist fiction will always be in demand, one supposes, given the tendency of real life to remain bloody.

Sigh, and sink teeth into rock solid old crust of sourdough rye bread. Agonising stab of pain racks me to the depth of my tooth and eye socket. Seize jaw and shriek for several seconds, but children symbiotically locked into Saturday morning TV and would remain oblivious were I to choke on muesli and crash blue and lifeless on to the cork-effect vinyl.

Teeth becoming a problem because of rampant recession (of gums, that is). For years now ice cream has had to be smuggled straight down without touching the sides: am I also to be denied the pleasure of chewing crusts? How am I to ingest nourishment? Long for nice savoury soufflé or perhaps a frail mouth-watering mousse. It strikes me that I might cadge an invite out of Elaine. Besides, I want to spy on her ménage with Tom, much as the poor moth is drawn to the flame. Seize telephone.

'Dulcie! What's new?' It is Tom himself who replies. Inform him that the answer to What's new is *Too much, by heaven*, and express the hope that our households might get together as Spouse is away in Brighton and I cannot hope to scale the heights of the weekend without oxygen and sherpas.

'Elaine's away too,' he confides. 'Gone to see her mum . . . why don't I come over and cook you that pasta thing with salmon?'

Heart leaps with foolish mixture of memory and anticipation. Inform it sternly that tonight could be the beginning of a much more rewarding relationship based on mutual respect, honesty, comfortable old affection, etc. Heart retorts, Sod that, let's hope for a grope.

Seething with sudden energy, announce to children I am taking them to Rusbridge Swimming Pool as secretly know that will tire them out. Water delightfully warm, though I am slightly perturbed as usual by the sight of immersed toddlers wearing nappies, and trust it will not lead to Swimming Poo. Kick madly in attempt to slim thighs perceptibly by 6.30, but pull muscle in knee. Limp to showers and discover I've left the anti-chlorine shampoo at home. Gnash teeth, and endure another paroxysm of pain. Must go to dentist.

Children swear horribly at having to crawl out on to dry land, as no doubt they did three million years ago. Harriet tearful at the thought that there aren't such things as mermaids or unicorns. Natural History cannot compete with Unnatural History, it seems. Must mention the concept of Unnatural History to Spouse when he returns from Brighton.

Lunch taken at Little Chef. Choose the soup, but exquisite pain convulses my jaw at the merest hint of anything hot, anything cold, or anything chewy. Order pot of tea and glass of cold water. Dilute hot tea with cold water, and wonder if increasing age will force one to other such heretical rituals. Half a pint of tepid tea, however, will probably prevent fainting in Tesco's. Though I wouldn't bet on it. Deep disapproval of supermarkets as a phenomenon does not prevent my spending £46.85 there.

Arrive home and fling myself on bed to rest jaw and knee. Aware that I pong of chlorine and that soon I must crank myself up and spend some time in front of bathroom mirror trying to make a silk purse out of a sow's ear. The billowing sounds of Walt Disney in the room below, however, lull me into a deep sleep from which I am awoken aeons later by Harriet jumping on my jaw and knee shouting 'Tom's come!'

Distraught to discover it is 6.30 and that as well as smelling of chlorine, I am crumpled, rumpled and disgruntled and a strange red weal of sleep has appeared across my face. Stumble downstairs and confront Tom, who grins at my dishevellment and says, 'Ah! The Curse of the Mummy's Tomb, I presume.' So much for the hope of a grope. Ancient History.

ninety-one

'Mummy! I think Jeremy Beadle is handsome, don't you?' Knowing Harriet's penchant for tenacious argument, I readily agree. Tom, cooking the pasta, shares an illicit grin with me. Wonder if we shall share anything more delectably illicit before the night is over. Tom appears to have abandoned his attempt at matrimony, defeated by Sabrina's KGB interrogations and by the loutish aggression of her large sons. What were Hector's heavies called? Myrmidons? And does anyone ever learn Latin and Greek these days?

'Why are you looking *sad*, Mummy?'

'Because nobody learns Greek any more.'

Am often accused of looking sad, these days, even when in a mood of beatific serenity. Suspect it is to do with the effect of gravity on my jowls. Gravity leads in time, to *gravitas*. Perhaps at the age of forty one should don sticky-soled shoes and walk upon the ceiling, like a fly.

'Penny for your thoughts,' Tom takes advantage of a pause in the cookery to come and sit at the kitchen table, where I am allegedly making a fruit salad.

'This kiwi's gone alcoholic.'

'I'll have it then!' roars Harriet, inserting herself between us. So Tom is still interested in me from the neck up. Well, it's a start. Forbid Harriet the kiwi, because of risk of diarrhoea, and suggest she might like to go and read the medical dictionary.

'Oh, whoopee!' she cries. 'I'll look up peonies!'

She runs off to the sitting room, where Henry is watching somebody being loudly killed. Ah, the peace of home life in the late twentieth century. Still, I suppose it beats being a Greek. At least my husband isn't being dragged around the walls of Troy by his heels.

'So: penny for them.' Tom leans in towards me and delivers what can only be described as a blinding leer. Essential I conceal from him the tepid scrambled egg which passes for my thought processes these days. Must be enigmatic. Attempt fleeting impersonation of Mona Lisa.

'No need to look so smug, just because my marriage is over.'

Startled by this blatant resumption of erotic badinage, though hurt that my enigma looked like smugness. But wait! *Am* I smug that his marriage is over?

'Why did you ever marry her in the first place?' I demand.

'To try to get over you, of course,' Tom grins, and seizing the hair on the back of my head, propels me towards his lips. A scalding hiss breaks out: is it my heart?

'The pasta's boiling over!'

'So am I.'

We kiss with ferocity for the first time for over two years. Even so, the literary editor in me suggests that 'So am I' is a rather trite cliché belonging to the bodice-ripping genre. Never mind! Sack the literary editor! Sod *scrutiny*! I want my bodice ripped!

'Stop!' I lie, fighting my way out of this clichéd clinch. 'They're not even in bed yet!'

Turn down the heat under the pasta as well. Harriet runs in with medical dictionary and invites us to examine diagram of a penile implant.

'Look what men have inside their peonies, Mummy! *Why?*'

'Goodness knows.'

'Can I have a look at yours, Tom?'

'Don't you dare speak to Tom like that!'

'Oooh! Snot fair! I want to go to a pub and see a stripper!'

Children are wrenched from their sex and violence, fed, and sent to bed. But the presence of Tom is disastrously exciting to them as well. He is ordered to read stories, tell jokes about willies, prove God exists, etc.

I seize the moment to apply moisturiser with the careless generosity of a bricklayer, tousle hair winsomely, and turn down the dimmer switches. Sniff armpits anxiously and detect onion soup. Sneak into bathroom and apply deodorant without undressing: essential late-twentieth-century skill akin to burglary. Arrange myself tastefully on sofa leafing through medical dictionary. Realise I have Erythema ('Redness of the skin . . . caused by blushing, hot flushes, raised temperature, inflammatory conditions . . .'). Wonder which Greek word

Erythema comes from. Try not to lose my cool, though recall that some like it hot, and hope Tom is one of them.

Ten seconds later he bounces down beside me, and grabs the medical dictionary.

'Just a second,' he says. 'What's the Greek for jock-itch?'

ninety-two

ATTEMPTING TO GET THROUGH December by watching videos and neglecting both everyday domestic duties and special seasonal ones.

'Mummy! Can I draw some people having sex?'

'Er – making love, you mean? Oh, all right. If you must. As long as you tear it up before Mrs Body comes on Monday.'

'Why?'

'Some people don't like that sort of thing.'

'But Mrs Body must have done it herself! Because of Tracey and Darren and Michelle!'

The really annoying thing is that heavy-handed censorship, in the form of a *grand et massif* NON, would have been so much more restful.

'I don't suppose you're going to make any mince pies?' asks Spouse with wan sigh suggesting I am guilty of nutritional impoverishment as well as moral laxity.

'Too bloody right I'm not,' I affirm, rewinding video to enjoy Gareth Edwards's try for the fifteenth time. See old Gareth get his try and you'll believe a man can fly.

'I'm not sure we can afford to go to Goa after all,' observes Spouse. Suspect this is veiled blackmail: mince pies or no holiday. Ignore the fact that I am financially dependent on him and could not, on my own, even afford a weekend in Warminster. Not sure whether to be repelled by the hint of War in Warminster, or attracted by the soupçon of Warm. Had started to go off Goa anyway, since I discovered it was once Portuguese and boasts the Basilica of Bom Jesus which houses the remains of St Francis Xavier, i.e. not really completely Indian after all. Portugal only too hot.

Bom Jesus also a bizarre name for somewhere in Asia. Recall M is Portuguese equivalent of N, as in *Cone imto the gardem*

Naud. So Bom Jesus is nothing to do with bums or bombs, but simply boring old Bon, as in Simon le Bon. Wonder if he is Portuguese like Joanna the Mad and Wilfred the Hairy. Rewind video for sixteenth time to admire Gareth the Airborne.

In 1973 men all had proper long hair: masses of Quattrocento curls, not the weaselly pony tails of nowadays. Point this out to Spouse, who threatens to grow a pony tail unless I make mince pies.

Eventually I am from the sofa untimely ripped by impudent phone. It is Elaine-over-the-road, who asks what Harriet and Henry and Spouse would like for Christmas. Promise to tell her later when they are not eavesdropping.

'I suppose you'd better ask her over,' sighs Spouse.

'What, for *Christmas*?' Although Elaine is more fun than any member of my family, and presumably will be home alone otherwise as her parents live in Australia, some primitive instinct urges me to give idea *grand et massif NON*. 'Oh all right then,' recover merry magnanimity with huge effort. 'Good idea, why not? She can make the mince pies.'

'I'm sick of Rugby: let's have Ian Botham slaughtering the Aussies back in – when was it?' Thank goodness for the video: thus a nation in decline can bask in past glories, tucked up in front of the hot air duct. If they'd had videos in the fifteenth century, Henry V could have watched himself winning the Battle of Agincourt over and over again instead of having to make do with Kenneth Branagh.

Discover that Goa has thirty-one inches of rain in July and that meningitis vaccinations are advised. That does it. Confide anxieties to Spouse who observes that if I had been Christopher Columbus we'd never have discovered Swindon. Can't help thinking that might have been an improvement. Leafing through the travel brochure, discover, at only £2500-odd, the Silk Route, taking in Samarkand, the Gobi Desert, the Flaming Mountains, the Great Wall of China, the Yellow River, Tashkent and Shanghai. Luckily we can't go for this one because of Tiananmen Square.

Nagging fear: if I invite Elaine for Christmas, will Tom, as her lodger, have to come too? Have developed strange disinclination to see him again after our brief coda a couple of weeks ago, whilst Spouse was in Brighton. Mrs Body is damned right: the second cup of tea is never as good as the first. But I always ignore her advice and have another cup, and it's always stewed.

'Mummy! Will you take us to the Leisure Centre?'

Though tempted by the idea of the Gobi Desert and the Flaming Mountains, I cannot face the half-mile trek to Rusbridge Leisure Centre. Insist I must lie on the sofa for a bit longer – i.e. until Leisure Centre closes.

At bedtime, step on to bathroom scales and discover that I have become what the Portuguese might call a *grand et massif Mom*.

ninety-three

DREAM I AM BACK at university and about to sit Finals again but have not read any of the books. Awake to find truth is almost worse: i.e. Christmas is upon us together with deadline for Bonkbuster, terminally stalled. And tonight must attend Harriet's end-of-term Parents' Evening – alone, since Spouse has important prior engagement. It must be odd to be called James Prior. One couldn't really make the most of one's name until retirement.

Whilst waiting to see Harriet's teacher, Mr Lamb, am entertained by the contents of her writing book. 'My Daddy is a lecherer' is hardly a monument to infantile perspicacity or philology. Recall various dons who also had problems discriminating between lechery and lecturing.

Odd, the pupil-teacher thingie. Local paper has revealed court case involving fourteen-year-old boy and female teacher aged forty-seven. If I find thirtyish Tom jejune, her little protégé must've been jejejejejune. Suddenly notice I have a ladder in my black tights. This is Harriet's fault for saying, 'Please, Mummy . . . don't wear trousers and put a bit of lipstick on and don't say anything silly.' Was bound to sink before this massive triple challenge to my habitual eccentric *déshabillé*.

'Hello, lovely to see you, how are you? I'm so glad you could make it.'

Thus I am welcomed, with broad grin, by Harriet's teacher Christopher Lamb. Despite the suggestion of effete eighteenth-century insanity implied by his name, I am glad to see he is of the Neanderthal tendency. I have always warmed to the prognathous: something to do with Mick Jagger dominating my deformative years. I was jaggered. Like jiggered only more so. Jiggered, jaggered or for those trying to negotiate middle age in trainers, joggered. Or for the lucky few elevated to the upper middle class, Jaegered.

We agree that Harriet must shut up, tidy up and shape up if she is to aspire to the subhuman. Then he asks when he may expect the pleasure of a sequel to my recent Bonkbuster *Birches*, in which Charlotte Beaminster makes the painful transition from Countess to Comrade. Admit I am stuck with my next *œuvre*, in which Fanny Hoddle is half-heartedly pursuing her erstwhile teacher Gertrude Lillywhite across southern Europe.

'Why stuck?'

'She hasn't met an interesting man since Dougal MacPravity.'

'But why does she have to meet a man for things to take off?'

'Er – well, that's the way things are in pulp fiction.'

Am then given stimulating tutorial about sexism and literature. Why is it that learning always delightful when it occurs informally, and only begins to be tedious when timetables are involved? Patten could end truancy at a stroke by making it compulsory. Then they'd all bunk off back to school. Or, in the case of sexually precocious fourteen-year-olds, bonk off.

'What have you enjoyed most on TV this autumn?' asks Mr Lamb.

'Well, apart from Ian Richardson, the wartime kitchen thing, I suppose.' Lies of course. What I've really enjoyed most is *Bottom*.

'Well, rehash that. Richardson as well if you like. And anything else you fancy. The creative process as compost heap.'

Diverted by the idea of rehashing *The Wartime Kitchen*, which is all about rehashing anyway.

So grateful for this suggestion, am tempted to put Christopher Lamb in Bonkbuster. Rehashed as Kit Agnew perhaps. But no. Unfair. On the way home, am tossed about like autumn leaf in the wake of overtaking container truck.

Juggered. Arrive – miraculously – to find children playing snakes and ladders with Tracey Body . Harriet cries, 'What did Mr Lamb say about me?' Reply, 'We agreed you were quite ghastly.' Beg ten minutes' leave to resuscitate the Bonkbuster, and fly to study, where dust on MSS several mms thick.

Nellie Hoddle looked up from her pig's bottom. Her mild china-blue eyes returned to the Carte Postale Fanny had sent from Nice: 'I miss your haslet Mother – and I'd give anything for a slice of your fried stump.' If I render this pig's buttock, she pondered, stuff it wi' Richardson's acid drops, an' pickle it wi' shoddy sweepings, 'appen it'll reach our lass in that thar Nice place before it's finished sweatin'.

Her husband strode into the kitchen, spat into the stone sink, and flung a handful of slugs into the cracked enamel bowl. 'Them thar slugs is up,' he reported laconically. Mrs Hoddle could not believe her luck. Fresh slugs, at this time of year! 'Thanks be,' she murmured, reverently.

ninety-four

It was nightfall in Berpsover. Nellie Hoddle drew the Crimean Plaid curtains and lit the oil lamp, pausing for a moment to caress the shining metal.

'It's coom oop reet well wi' that spot o'Attenborough's Monkey Brand Brass Buffer,' she pondered, then turned back to her suet. Expertly her worn old fingers folded in the Bowles's Royal Oats, chopped in the Brando Butter, scattered the raisins and a dash of Prince Edward's rum, then tied the basin up with muslin, secured it with a swatch of pit-pony's forelock, and set it to steam.

'What's tha fitherin' wi' now?' boomed her husband, loitering in the scullery to clean the grease off his clekkers with a handful of ash and a goose's gizzard.

'I'm just mekkin' one o' me puddens for our Fanny in France,' said Nellie. 'It'll fit in reet snug athwart t'corner o'yon box.' She smiled over her modest collection: a tin of Bottomley's humbugs, Old Bill's Whitewash for Reviving Soiled Knickers, a bottle of Shepherd's Tincture of Phosphorus for the Nerves, and a bar of Hurd's

Colonial Soft Soap. Should she include the Paisley comforter? Or was it too loud?

'I'm sendin' it all packed in one o'them hay-boxes, thisen, so t'pudden'll go on cookin' all t'way to t'St Tropez. Eee! I'm fair thorped wi'out me little Fanny . . . '

Fanny was not, however, as little as her mother remembered. Hundred of miles south, she dozed over her glass of Pssssschit, the hooks and eyes of her bodice gaping. She was heavily pregnant and obviously near her time. The supercilious waiter Fritz sighed, screwed up her unpaid bill and flicked it to the floor.

The door of the Café Freddo swung open, and a rawboned giant of a man stepped in out of the night. From the Barbarian north, thought Fritz, with a frisson of disgust.

'Can yez tell me th'way to th'Parc des Princes?' enquired the stranger. 'And am I still on th'Peripherique, at all?'

His grin was roguish and his voice, broguish. Fanny awoke with a start: the newcomer seemed suddenly to recognise her, prostrated himself, and seized her knees.

''Tis ye!' he ejaculated. 'I was told in a dream – by St Terry – to go to the aid of a maid in the south – he said they'd send a star, but bejasus! You've to keep your eyes on the road hereabouts entirely at all.'

'But who are you,' faltered Fanny. 'And er – what are you?'

'They call me a Flanker,' he confided.

'Oh, but I'm sure they don't really mean it!' cried Fanny pityingly. 'And you're kind to offer help, but I'm pregnant – and penniless, and homeless and hungry, and I haven't had a bath since Aix.'

'I'll tackle anything!' promised her saviour. 'I'm famous for it, darlin'. Me name is Seamus Flaherty.'

'Shameless Flattery?' Fanny trembled with the effort of comprehension. If only St Terry could have sent someone from Berpsover.

'Garçon fella!' called Seamus. 'Deugh Café O'Lait, et deugh Perty Pain O'Chocolat. An' a room for th'lady for th'night.'

'Je suis desolé, M'sieur,' lisped Fritz admiring Seamus's huge shoulders, 'mais nous sommes complets. A cause de Noel.'

'Well bring Noel here!' thundered Seamus, 'An' oi'll kick th'bastard past the twenty-five an' into the middle o' next year.'

Soon they were accommodated in a garage where the café owner normally kept his Lagonda. Suddenly, with a teeny shriek, Fanny went into labour.

'I'll be equal to this darlin', don't fret!' promised Seamus. 'Get yer head down and give it a heave! I've seen th'way old Geraint used to get th'ball out o'th'scrum: obstetric, 'twas to be sure entirely.'

A star blazed over St Tropez: a babe's cry rose, and a heavenly choir boomed: 'His name shall be called Wonderful, Counsellor, Almighty God, the Everlasting Father, the Prince of Peace.'

'No it won't!' cried Fanny indignantly. 'It's a girl, and she's going to be Nelly, after our mother.'

Owing to the eccentricities of Mrs Hoddle's handwriting, the hay-box had gone to Sarajevo, not St Tropez, where it exploded in the street just as an Archduke was riding past, causing the First World War. But that's another story.